Learning About Letters

Alphabet Cut and Paste

by Marilynn G. Barr

LAB201318
Learning About Letters
ALPHABET CUT AND PASTE
by Marilynn G. Barr

Published by: Little Acorn Books™
Originally published by: Monday Morning Books, Inc.

Entire contents copyright © 2013 Little Acorn Books™

Little Acorn Books
PO Box 8787
Greensboro, NC 27419-0787

Promoting Early Skills for a Lifetime™

Little Acorn Books™
is an imprint of Little Acorn Associates, Inc.

http://www.littleacornbooks.com

Permission is hereby granted to reproduce student materials in this book for non-commercial individual or classroom use. *School-wide or system-wide use is expressly prohibited.

ISBN 978-1-937257-36-1

Printed in the United States of America

Contents

Introduction 4
Booklet Covers 5
I Can Cut and Paste Worksheets
    ABC 7
    DEF 8
    GHI 9
    JKL 10
    MNO 11
    PQR 12
    STU 13
    VWX 14
    YZ 15
    abc 16
    def 17
    ghi 18
    jkl 19
    mno 20
    pqr 21
    stu 22
    vwx 23
    yz 24

Cut and Paste Alphabet Posters
    Aa 25
    Bb 26
    Cc 27
    Dd 28
    Ee 29
    Ff 30
    Gg 31
    Hh 32
    Ii 33
    Jj 34
    Kk 35
    Ll 36
    Mm 37
    Nn 38
    Oo 39
    Pp 40
    Qq 41
    Rr 42
    Ss 43
    Tt 44
    Uu 45
    Vv 46
    Ww 47
    Xx 48
    Yy 49
    Zz 50

Cut and Paste Puzzles 51
Puzzle Board 64

Introduction

Reinforce alphabet skills with the cut and paste worksheets, mini-posters, and puzzles in *Alphabet Cut & Paste*, one of four in our *Learning About Letters* series.

Cut and Paste Worksheets
Provide crayons, scissors, and glue for children to complete worksheets (pages 7–24).

Cut and Paste Posters
Provide children with crayons, scissors, and glue to complete mini-posters (pages 25–50). Display completed posters in your classroom.

I Can Cut and Paste Booklets
Make construction paper folders to store each child's cut and paste worksheets. Provide each child with a booklet cover (pages 5–6) to color, cut out, and paste to the front of his or her folder. Write each child's first initial and name on the cover. Cut off the tops of completed worksheets and staple the lower parts inside folders to display at open house.

Alphabet Puzzle Gallery
Reproduce one puzzle board (page 64) on sturdy paper for each child. Provide each child with crayons, a puzzle board, and a cut and paste puzzle (pages 51–63). Show children how to color, cut apart, assemble, and glue the puzzle pieces to the puzzle board. Display completed puzzles on an Alphabet Puzzle Gallery bulletin board in your classroom.

An Alphabet Picnic (cover)
Prepare a picnic area with a blanket and a picnic or other type of basket filled with cut and paste puzzles and puzzle board place mats for a skills practice center. Reproduce the cut and paste puzzles and four puzzle boards (pages 51–64) on sturdy paper. Color and cut out the puzzles and puzzle boards. Store matching puzzle pieces in separate resealable plastic bags. Color four large sheets of construction paper to resemble checkered picnic place mats. Glue the puzzle boards to the place mats. Store the place mats and puzzles in the basket. Encourage children to work in pairs to assemble and identify the picture and the beginning letter sound for each completed puzzle.

Booklet Cover

I Can Cut and Paste the Alphabet

_____
Name

Booklet Cover

I Can Cut and Paste the Alphabet

_____
Name

I Can Cut and Paste
A, B, and C

Name _____

Cut out the letters.
Paste each letter under the picture that matches.

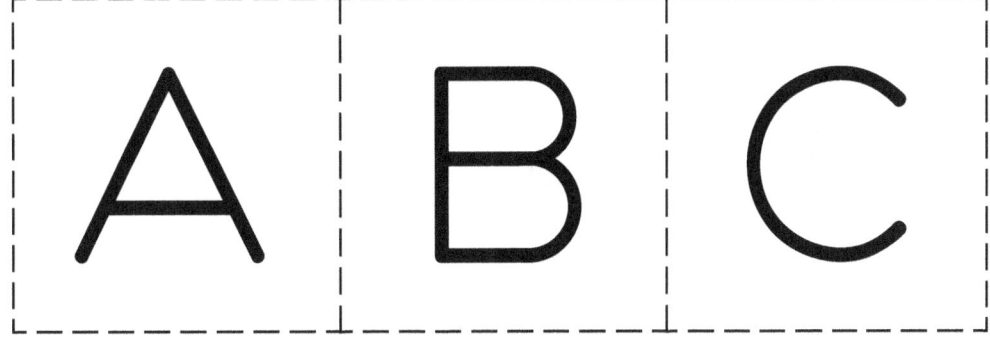

A B C

I Can Cut and Paste
D, E, and F

Name _____

Cut out the letters.
Paste each letter under the picture that matches.

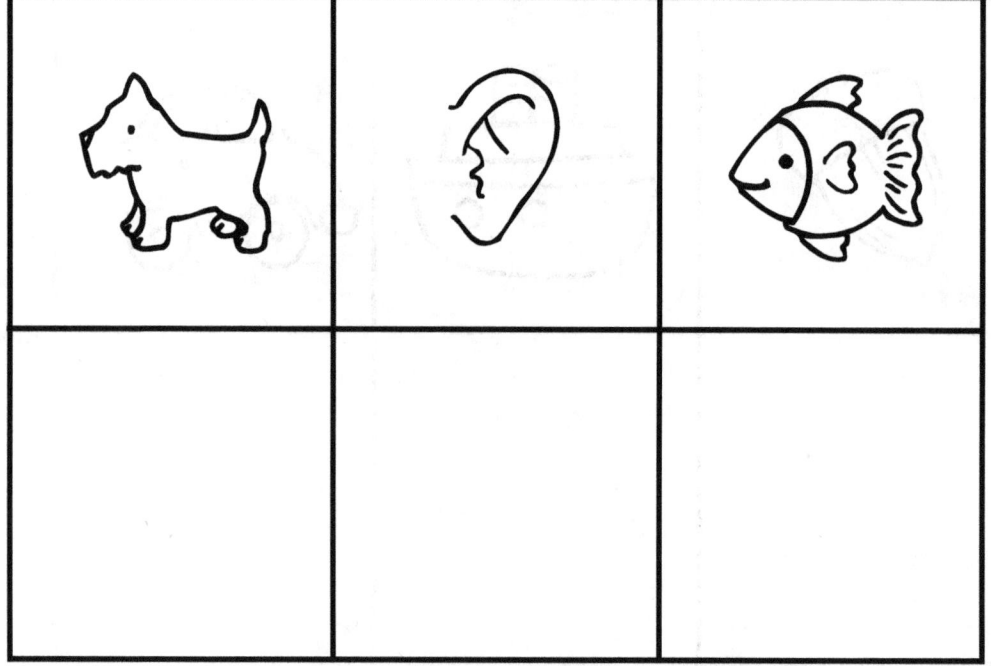

D E F

I Can Cut and Paste
G, H, and I

Name _____

Cut out the letters.
Paste each letter under the picture that matches.

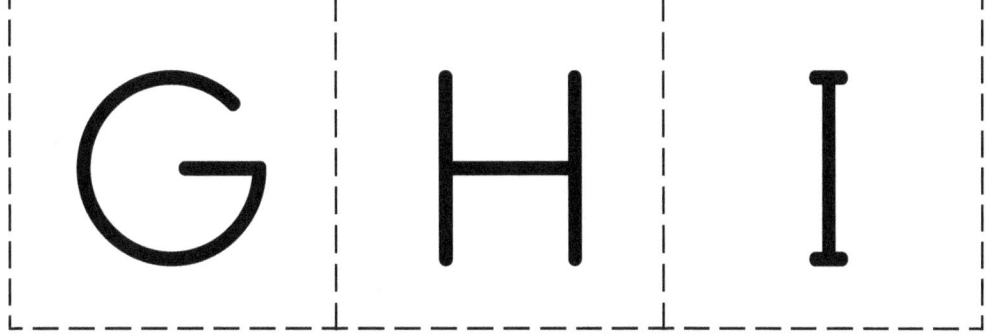

I Can Cut and Paste J, K, and L

Name _____

Cut out the letters.
Paste each letter under the picture that matches.

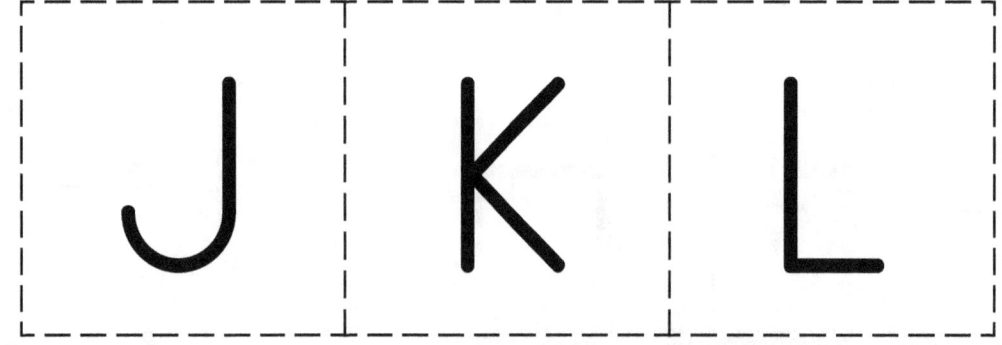

J   K   L

I Can Cut and Paste
M. N, and O

Name _____

Cut out the letters.
Paste each letter under the picture that matches.

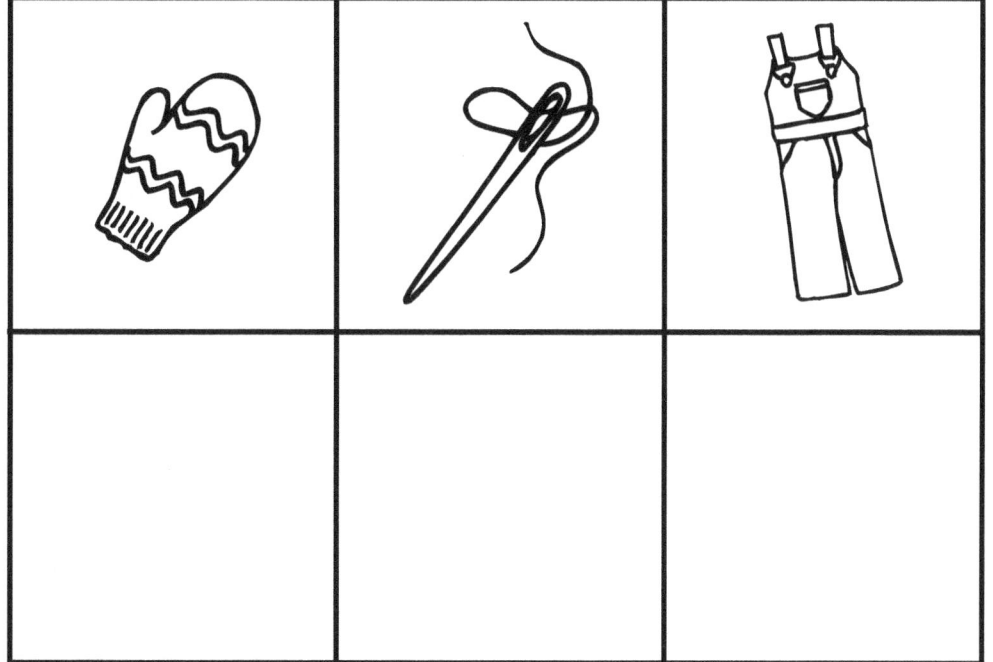

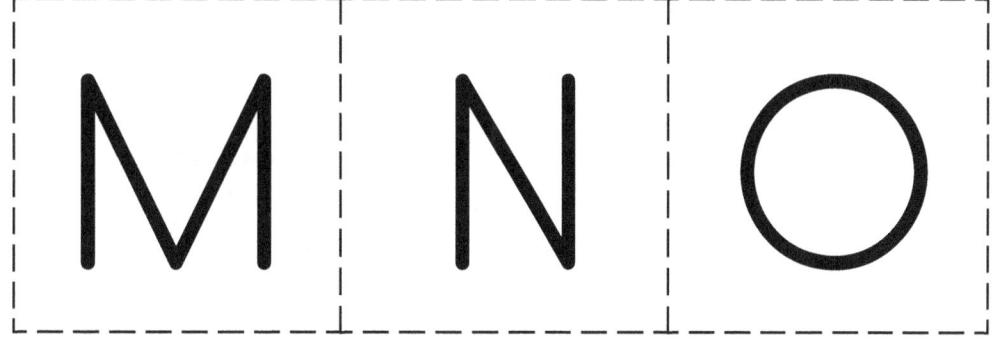

I Can Cut and Paste
P, Q, and R.

Name _____

Cut out the letters.
Paste each letter under the picture that matches.

I Can Cut and Paste
S, T, and U

Name _____

Cut out the letters.
Paste each letter under the picture that matches.

S T U

I Can Cut and Paste
V, W, and X

Name _____

Cut out the letters.
Paste each letter under the picture that matches.

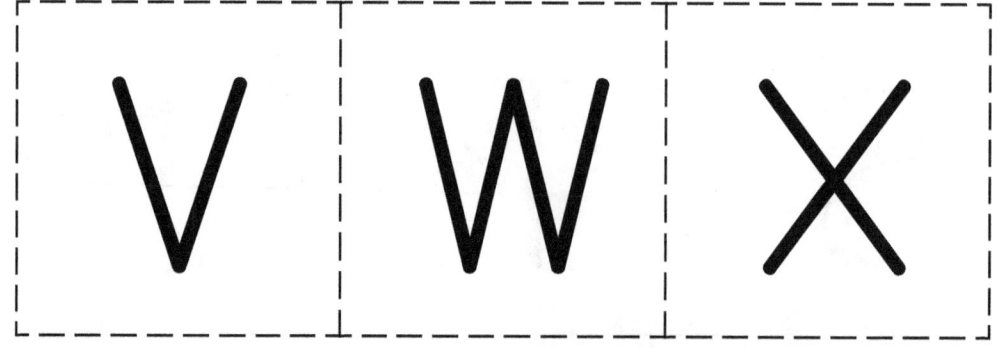

 # I Can Cut and Paste
Y and Z

Name _____

Cut out the letters.
Paste each letter under the picture that matches.

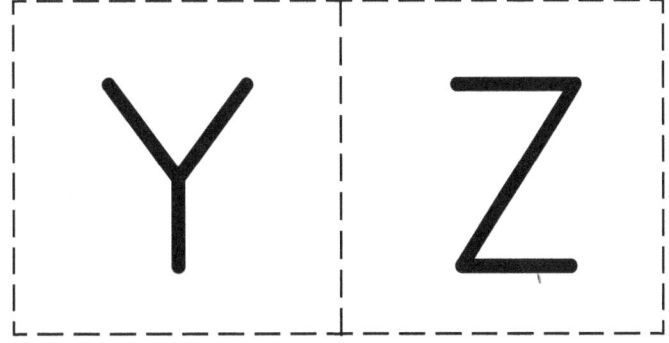

I Can Cut and Paste
a, b, and c

Name _____

Cut out the letters.
Paste each letter under the picture that matches.

a   b   c

I Can Cut and Paste
d, e, and f

Name _____

Cut out the letters.
Paste each letter under the picture that matches.

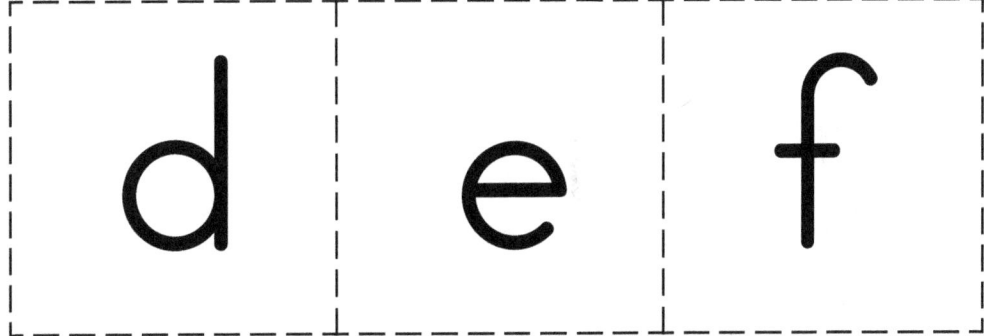

I Can Cut and Paste
g, h, and i

Name _____

Cut out the letters.
Paste each letter under the picture that matches.

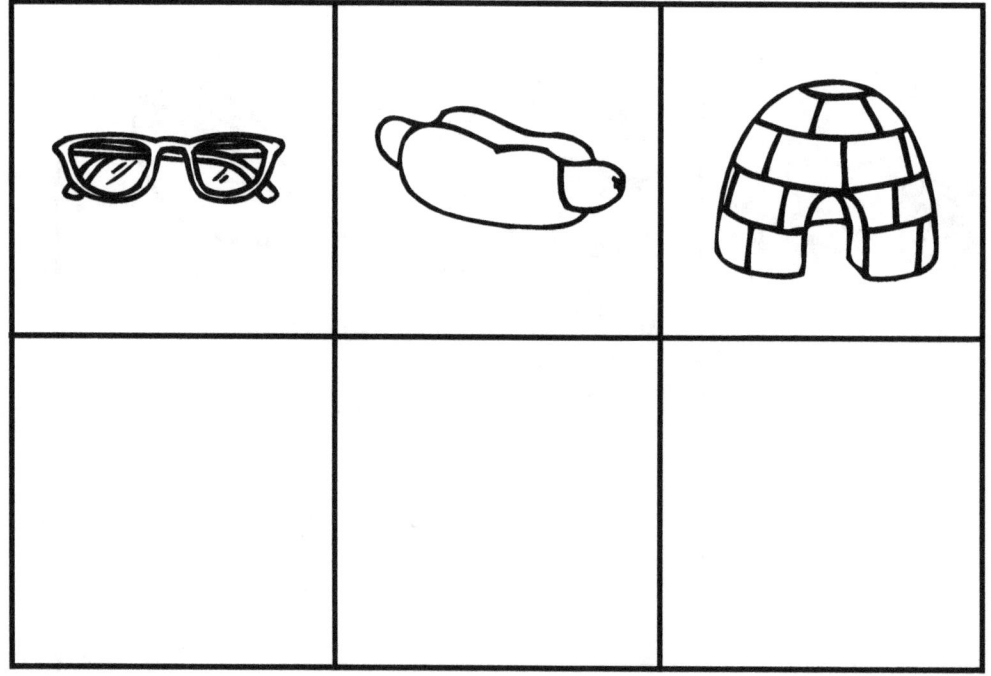

g h i

I Can Cut and Paste
j, k, and l

Name _____

Cut out the letters.
Paste each letter under the picture that matches.

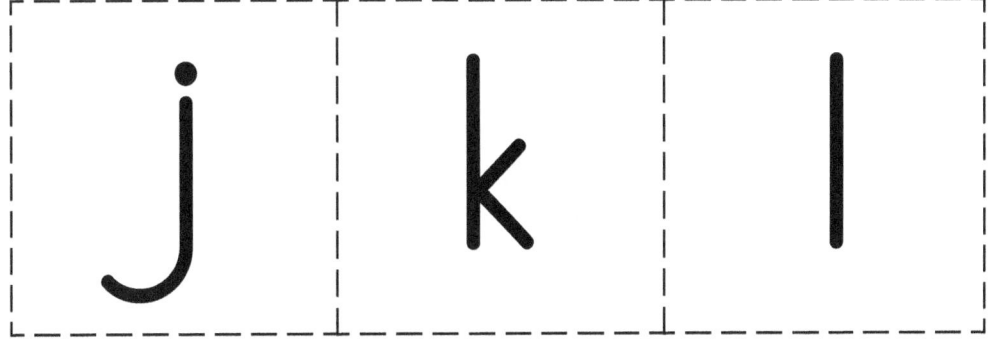

I Can Cut and Paste
m, n, and o

Name _____

Cut out the letters.
Paste each letter under the picture that matches.

| m | n | o |

 # I Can Cut and Paste
p, q, and r

Name _____

Cut out the letters.
Paste each letter under the picture that matches.

I Can Cut and Paste
s, t, and u

Name _____

Cut out the letters.
Paste each letter under the picture that matches.

s | t | u

I Can Cut and Paste
v, w, and x

Name _____

Cut out the letters.
Paste each letter under the picture that matches.

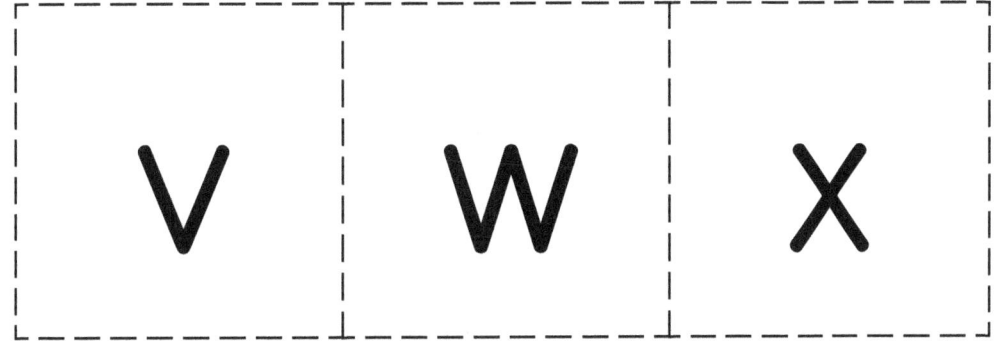

I Can Cut and Paste
y and z

Name _____

Cut out the letters.
Paste each letter under the picture that matches.

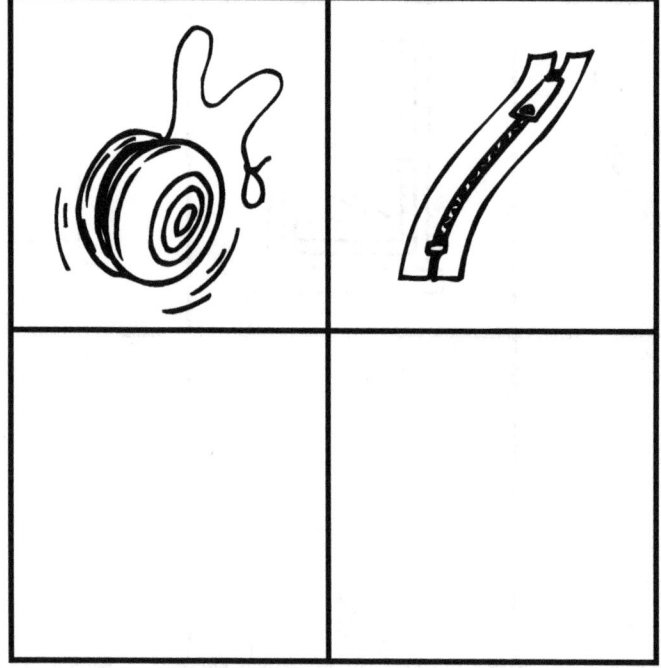

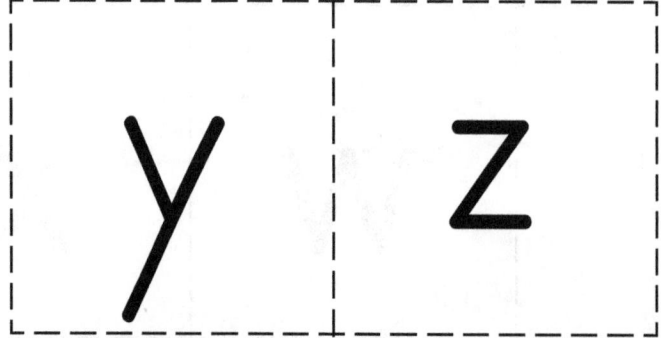

Cut and Paste Alphabet Poster

My Cut and Paste Alphabet Poster

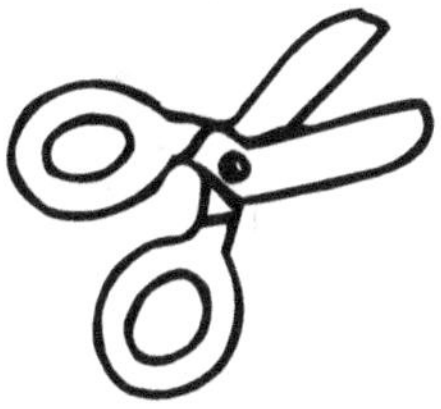

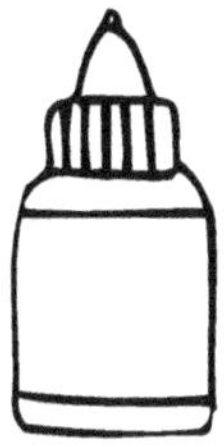

_____
Name

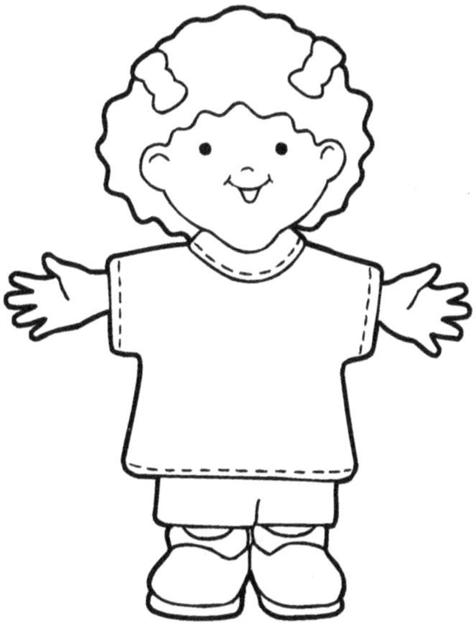

Cut and Paste Alphabet Poster

B	b		

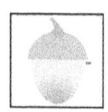

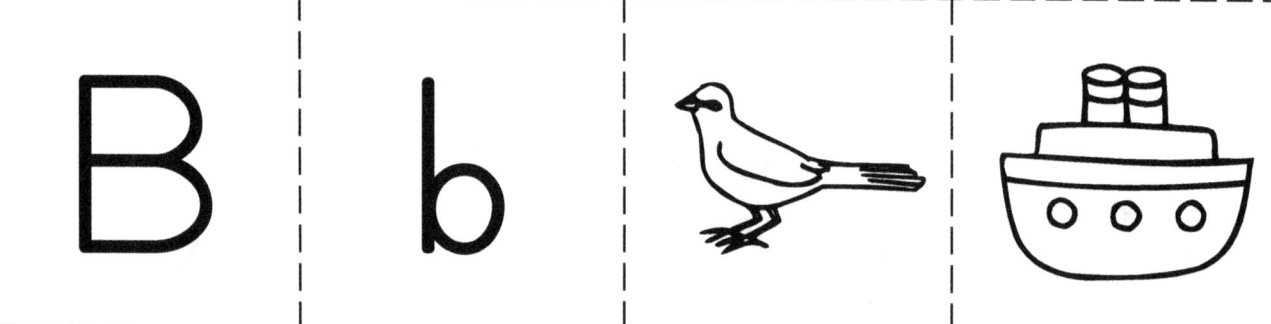

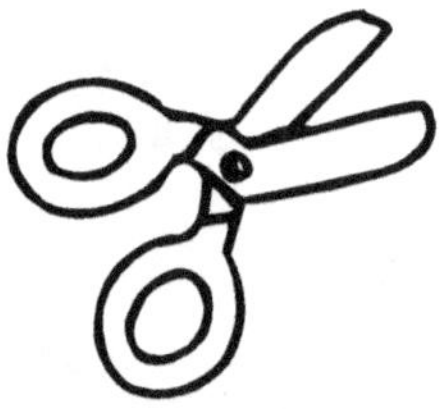

My Cut and Paste Alphabet Poster

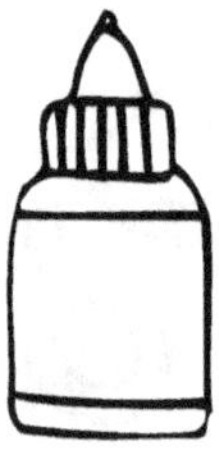

Name

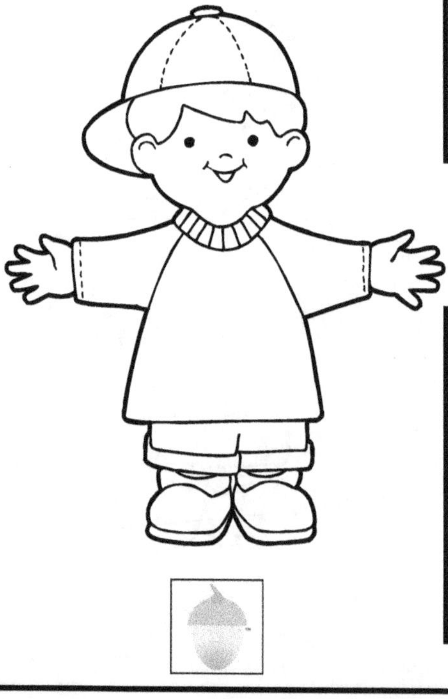

LAB201318 • ALPHABET CUT AND PASTE • 978-1-937257-36-1 •

Cut and Paste Alphabet Poster

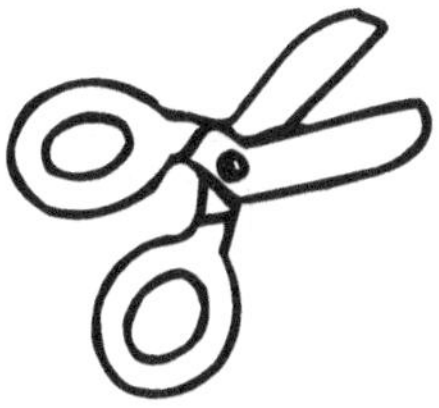

My
Cut and Paste
Alphabet Poster

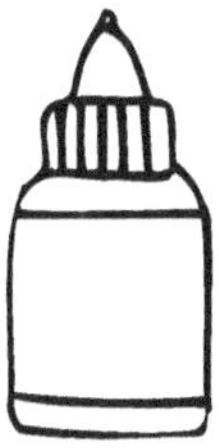

Name

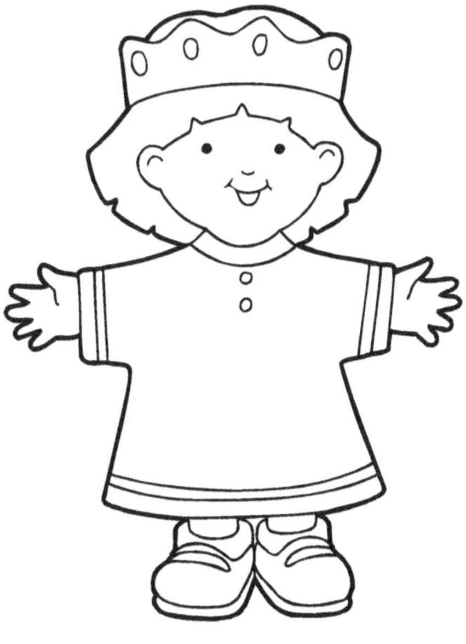

Cut and Paste Alphabet Poster

D

d

My Cut and Paste Alphabet Poster

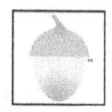

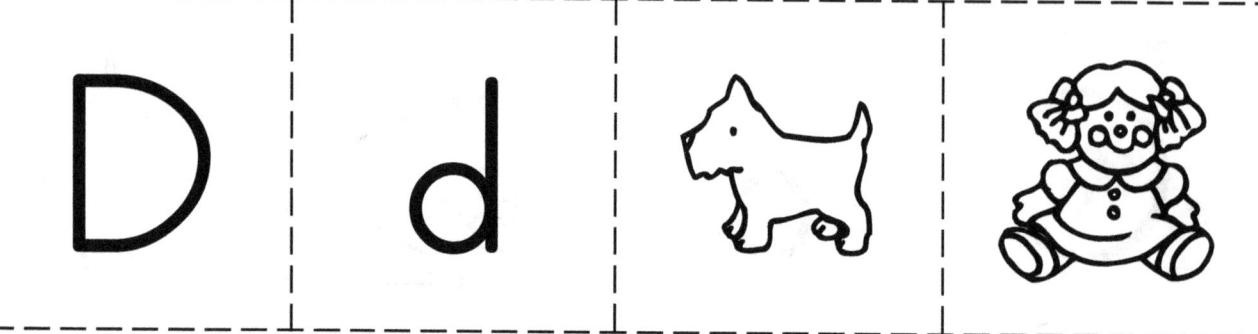

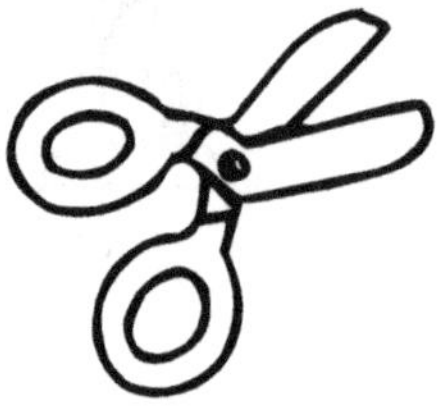

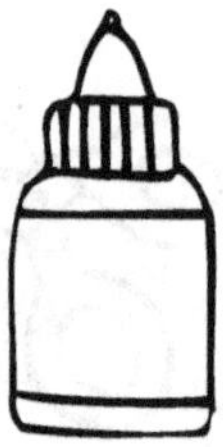

Name

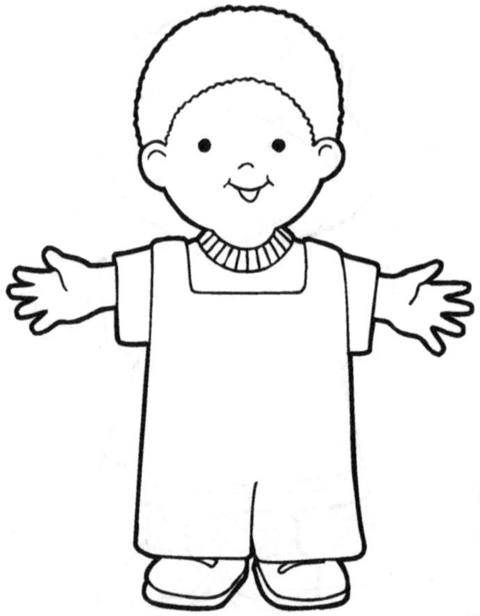

LAB201318 • ALPHABET CUT AND PASTE • 978-1-937257-36-1 • © 2013 Little Acorn Books™

Cut and Paste Alphabet Poster

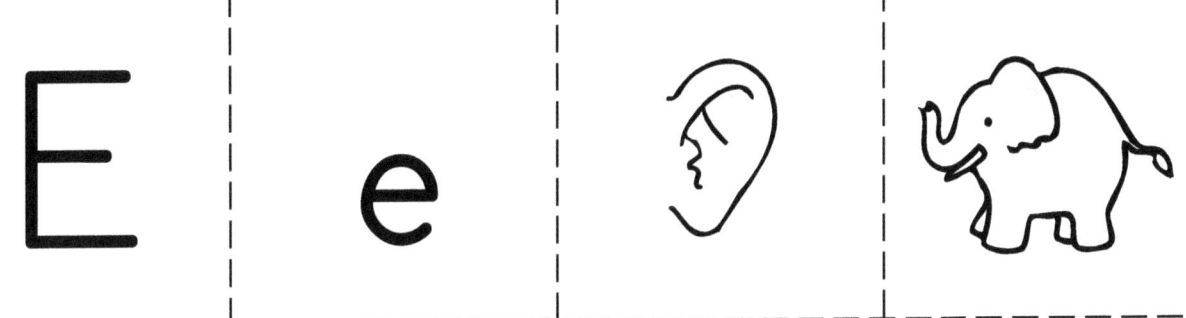

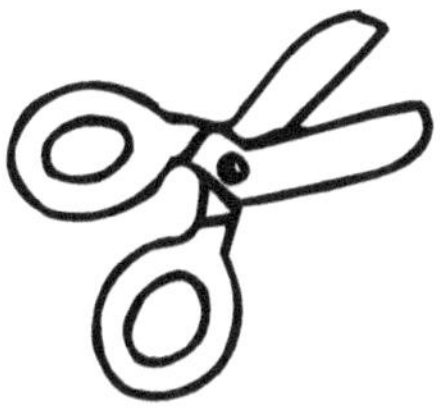

My Cut and Paste Alphabet Poster

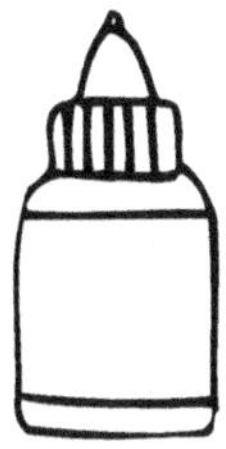

Name

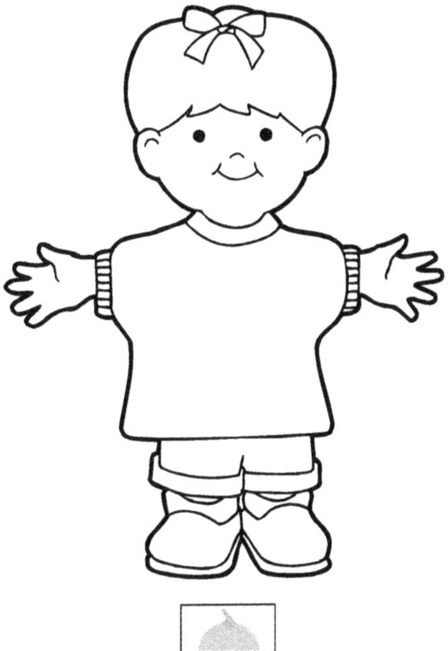

Cut and Paste Alphabet Poster

F	f		

My Cut and Paste Alphabet Poster

Name

Cut and Paste Alphabet Poster

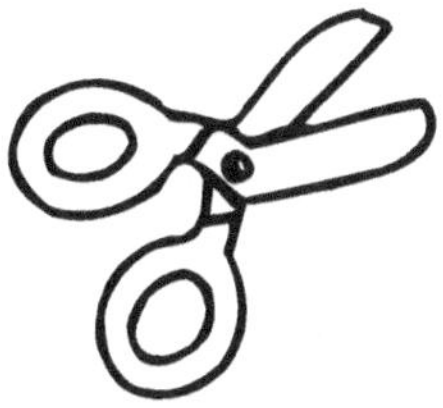

My
Cut and Paste
Alphabet Poster

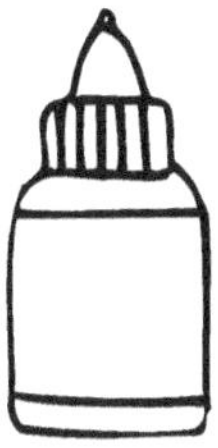

Name

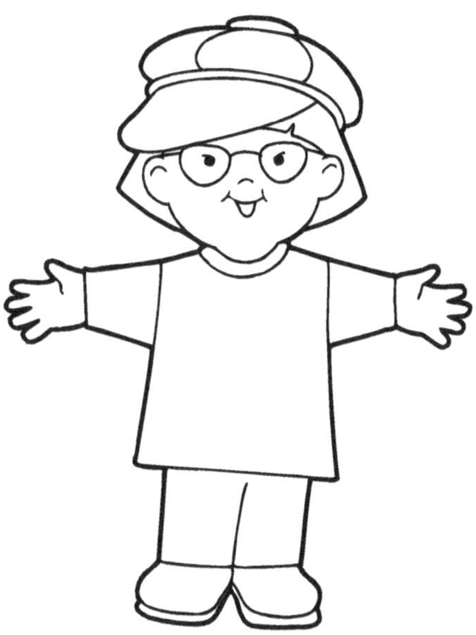

Cut and Paste Alphabet Poster

H

h

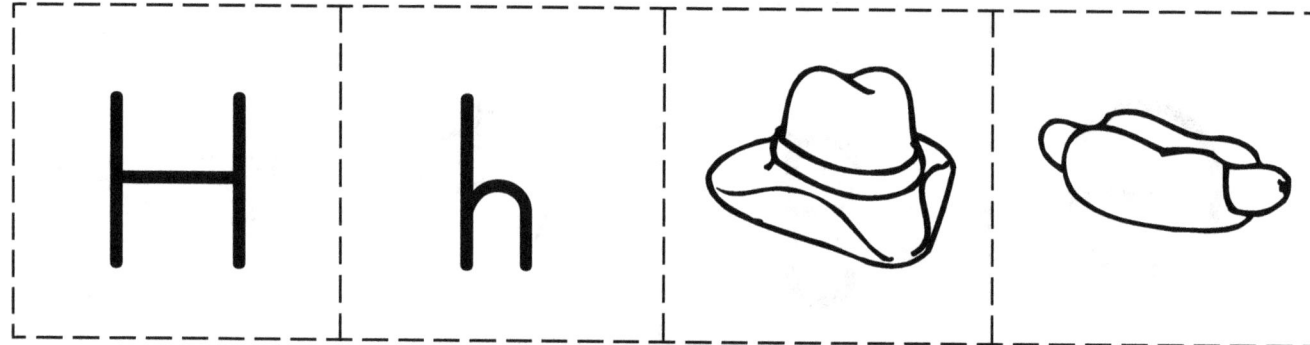

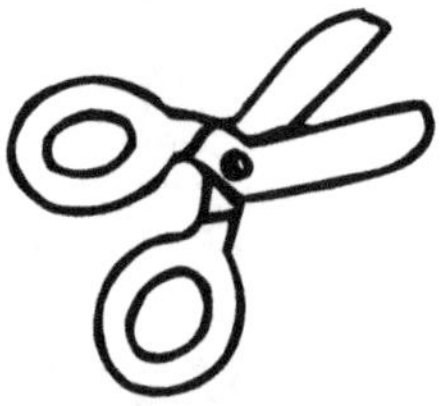

My Cut and Paste Alphabet Poster

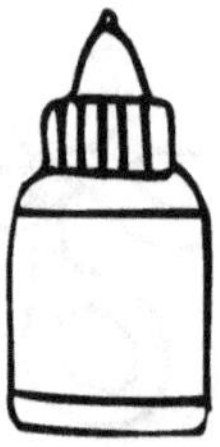

Name

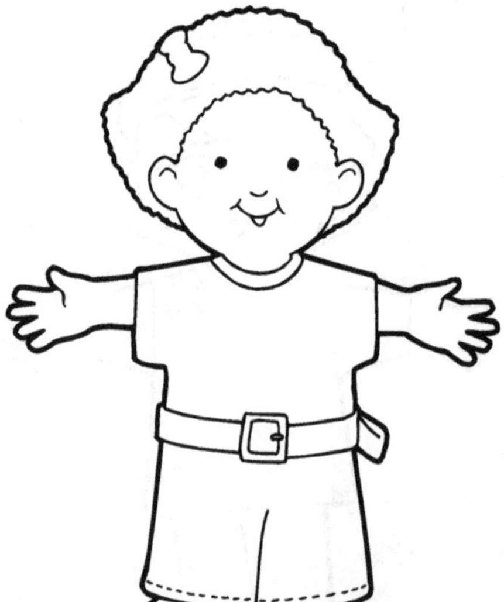

LAB201318 • ALPHABET CUT AND PASTE • 978-1-937257-36-1 •

Cut and Paste Alphabet Poster

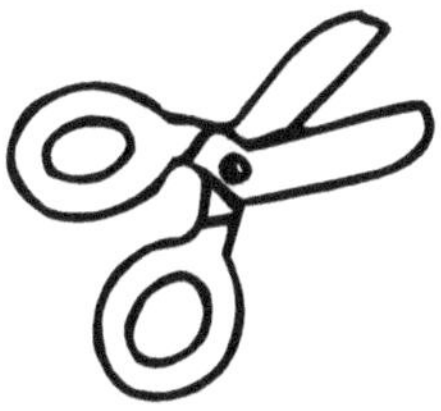

My Cut and Paste Alphabet Poster

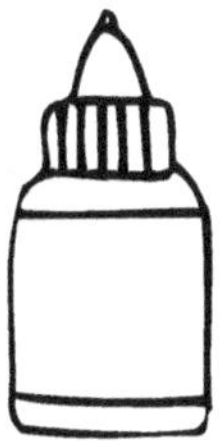

Name

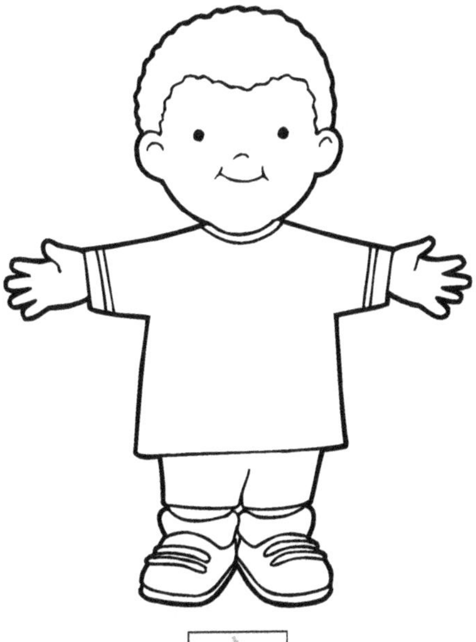

Cut and Paste Alphabet Poster

J

j

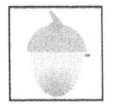

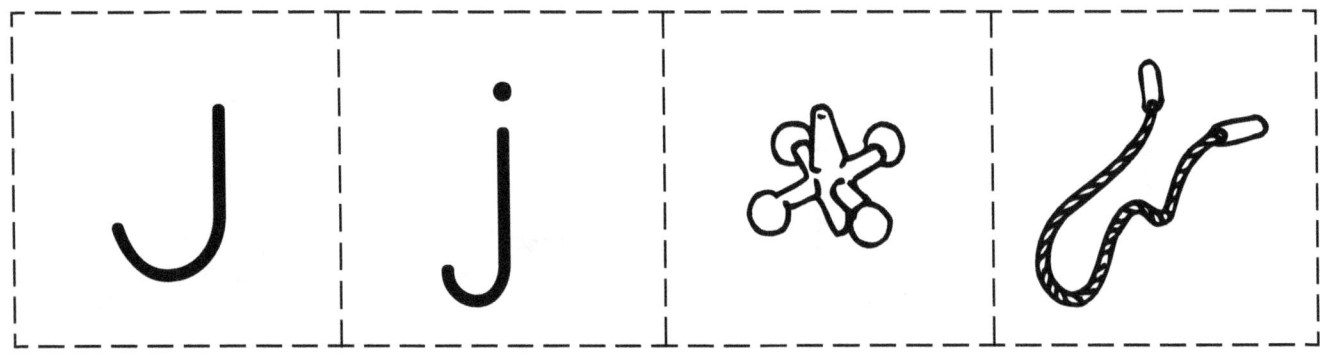

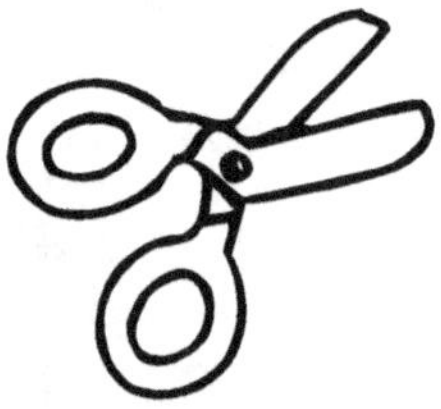

My
Cut and Paste
Alphabet Poster

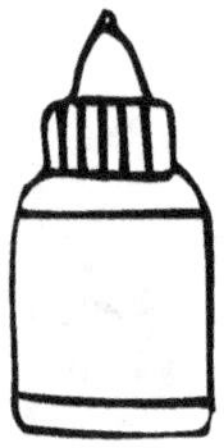

Name

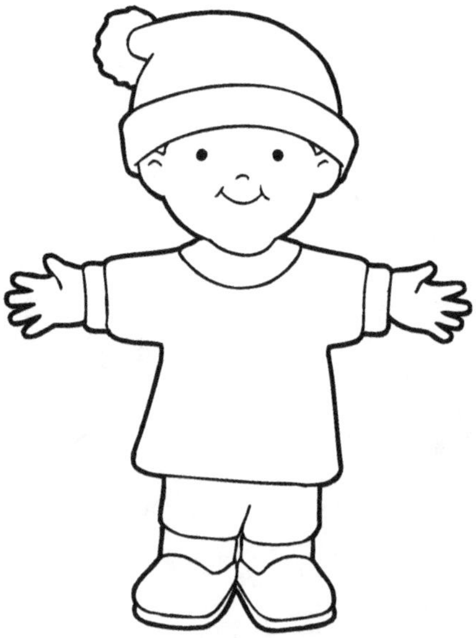

Cut and Paste Alphabet Poster

My Cut and Paste Alphabet Poster

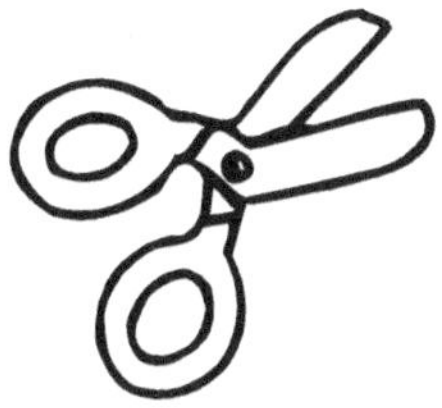

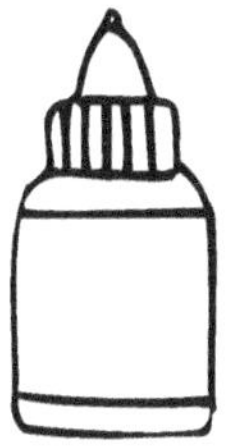

Name

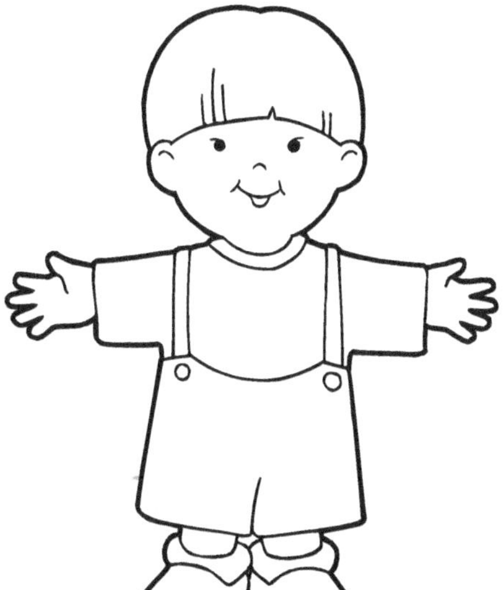

Cut and Paste Alphabet Poster

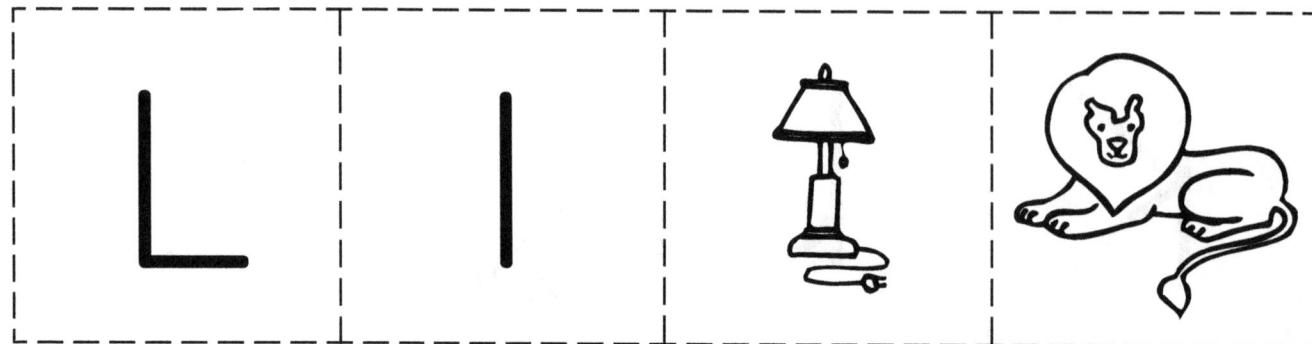

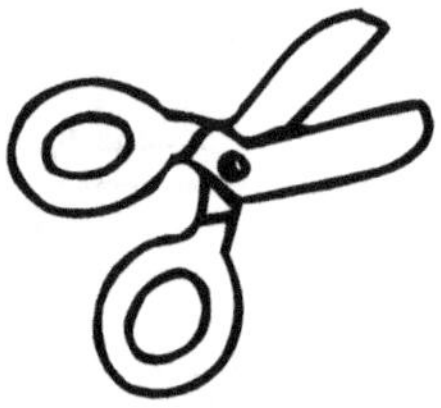

My
Cut and Paste
Alphabet Poster

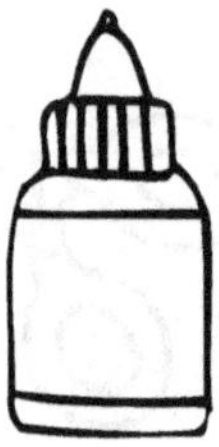

Name

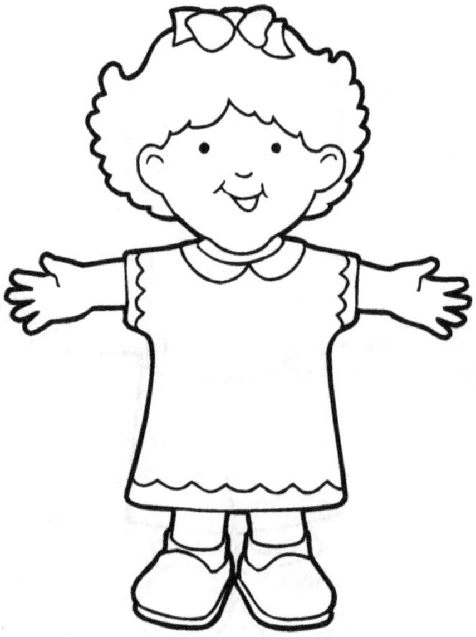

Cut and Paste Alphabet Poster

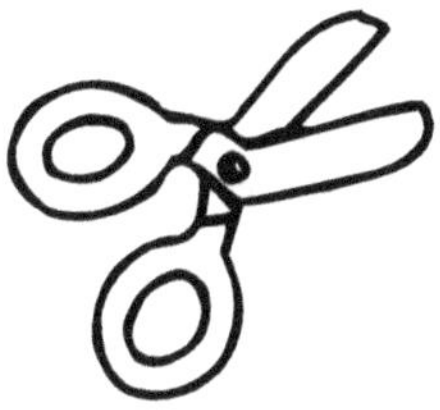

My
Cut and Paste
Alphabet Poster

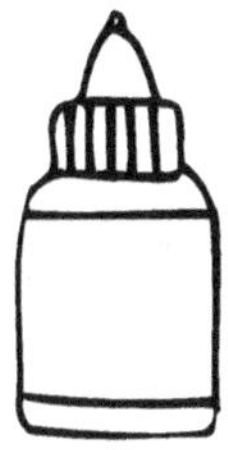

Name

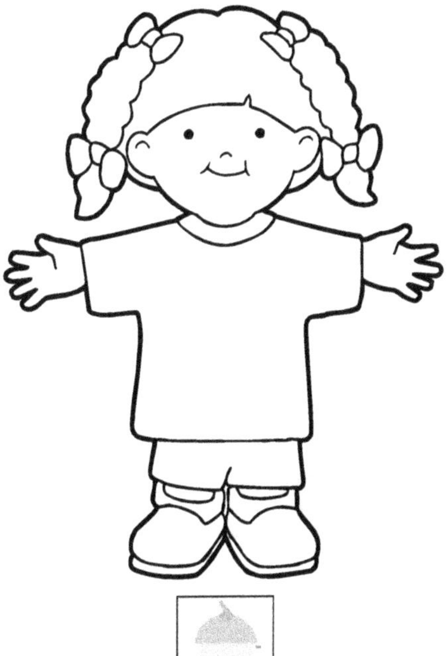

Cut and Paste Alphabet Poster

N n

My Cut and Paste Alphabet Poster

Name

Cut and Paste Alphabet Poster

O

o

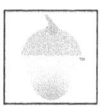

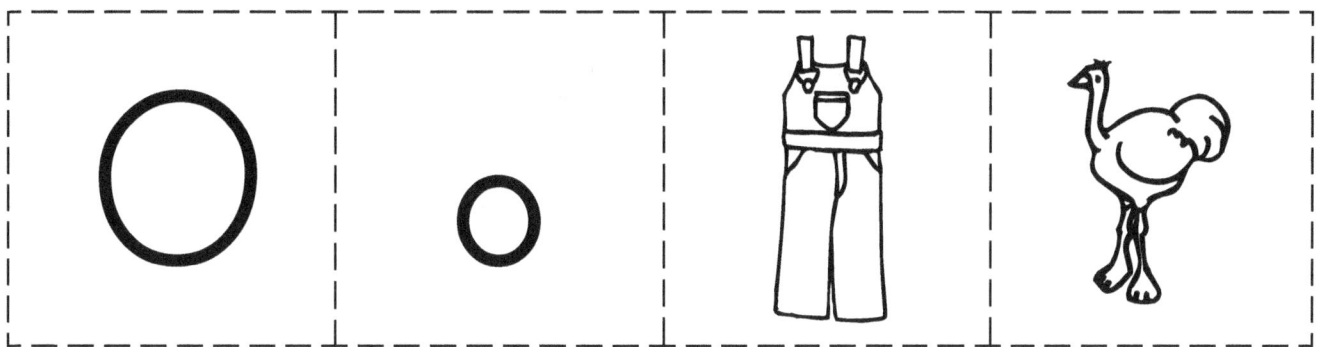

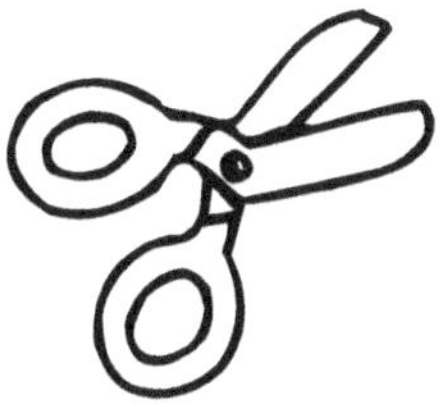

My Cut and Paste Alphabet Poster

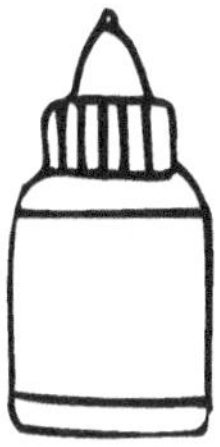

____

Name

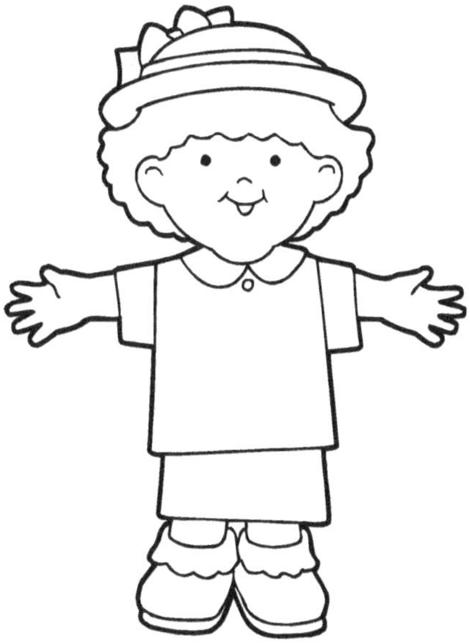

978-1-937257-36-1

Cut and Paste Alphabet Poster

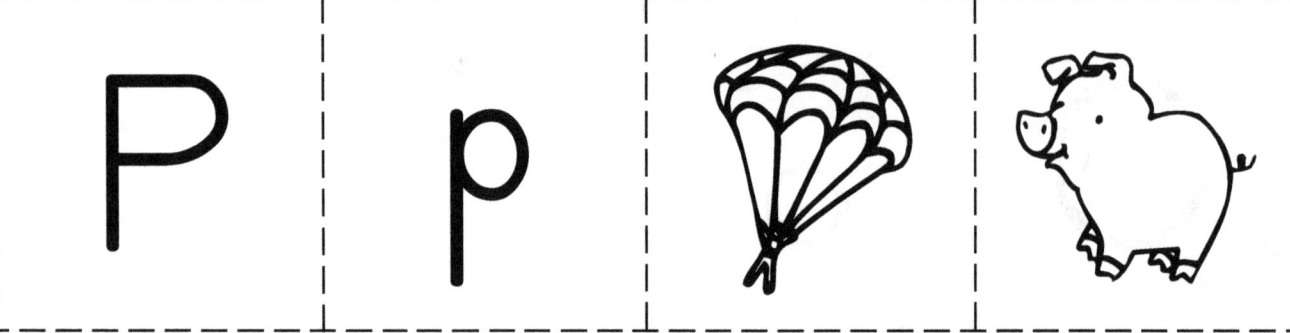

My Cut and Paste Alphabet Poster

_____
Name

40   LAB201318 • ALPHABET CUT AND PASTE • 978-1-937257-36-1 • © 2013 Little Acorn Books™

Cut and Paste Alphabet Poster

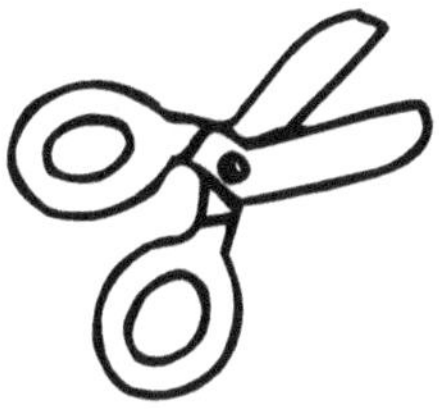

My Cut and Paste Alphabet Poster

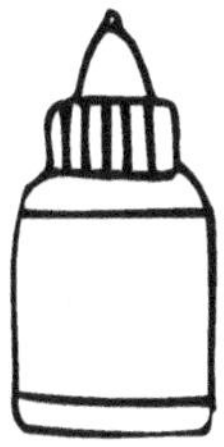

Name

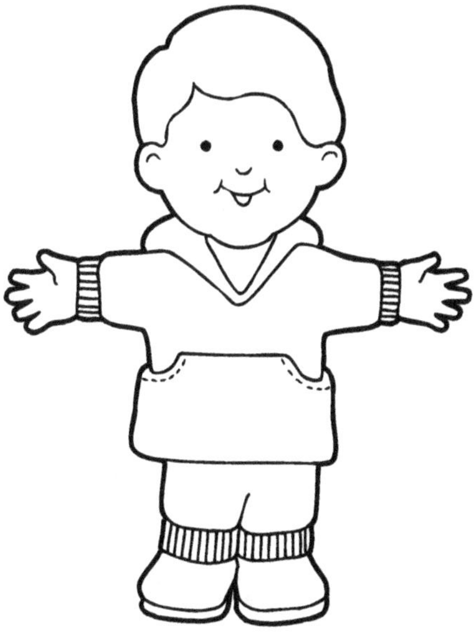

Cut and Paste Alphabet Poster

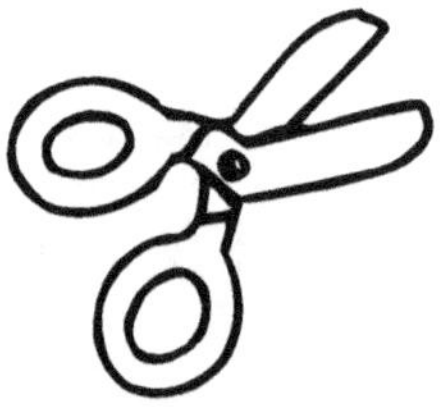

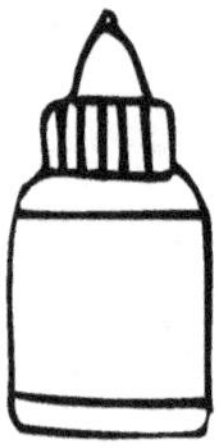

My Cut and Paste Alphabet Poster

Name

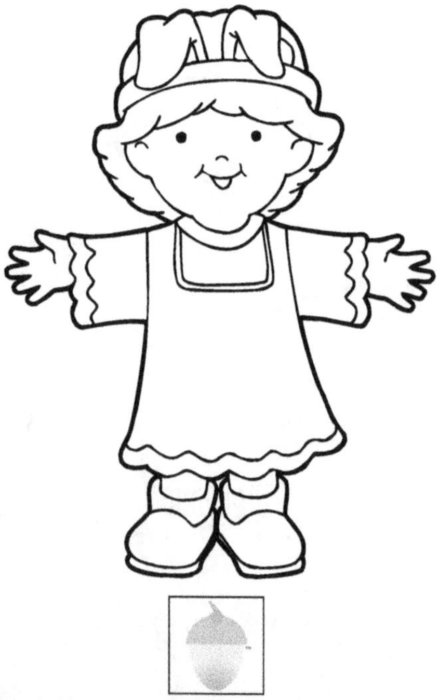

Cut and Paste Alphabet Poster

| S | s | ☃ | ★ |

My Cut and Paste Alphabet Poster

_____
Name

Cut and Paste Alphabet Poster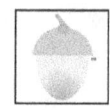

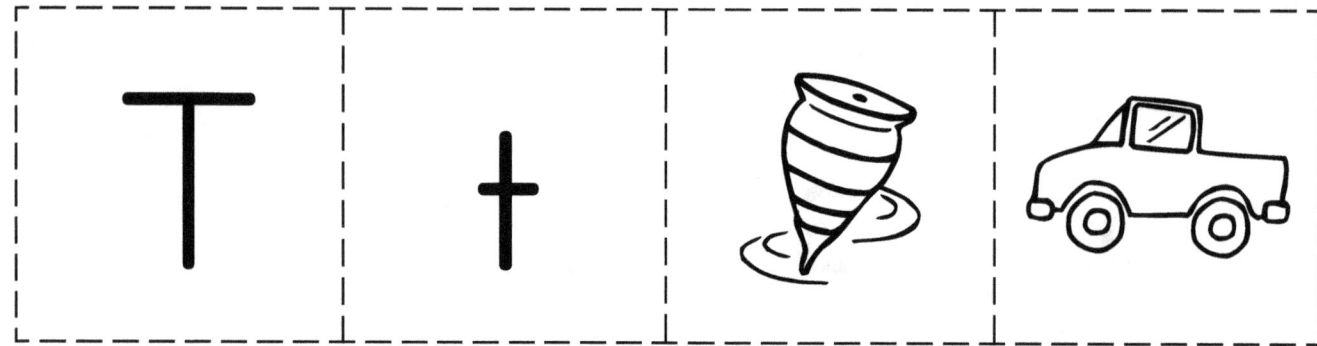

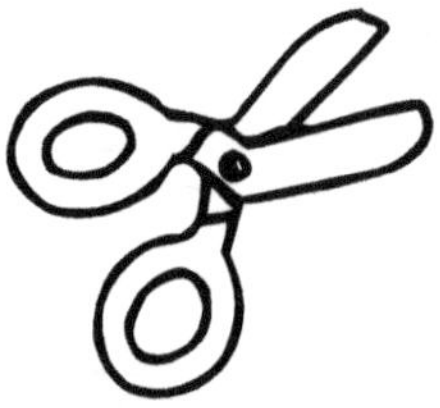

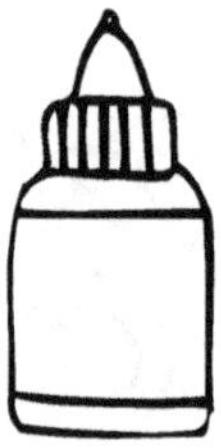

My Cut and Paste Alphabet Poster

Name

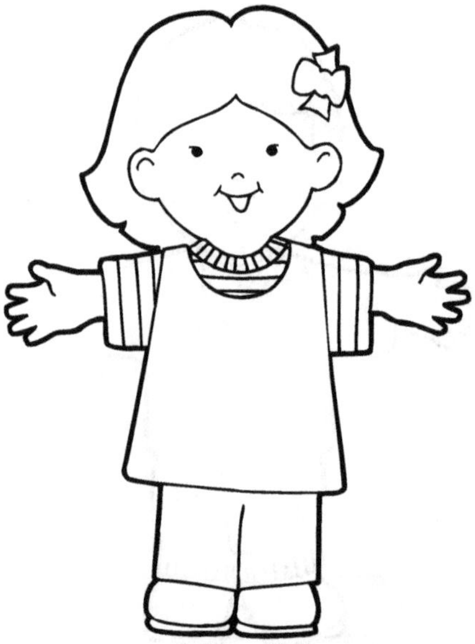

Cut and Paste Alphabet Poster

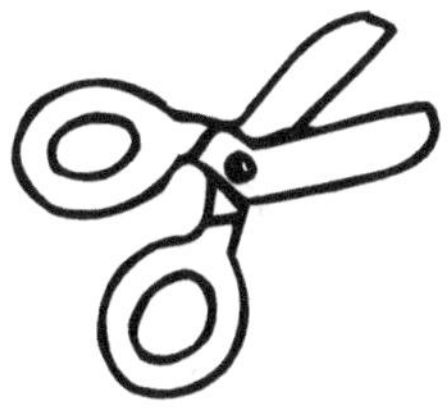

My
Cut and Paste
Alphabet Poster

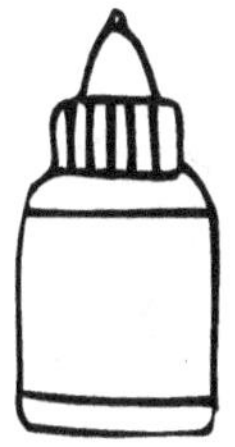

Name

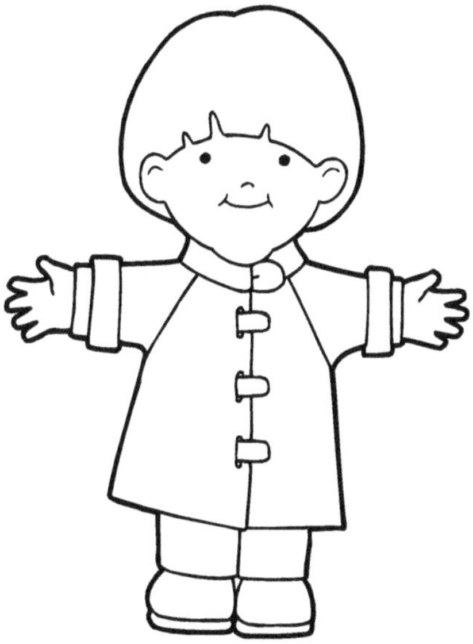

Cut and Paste Alphabet Poster

V

v

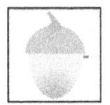

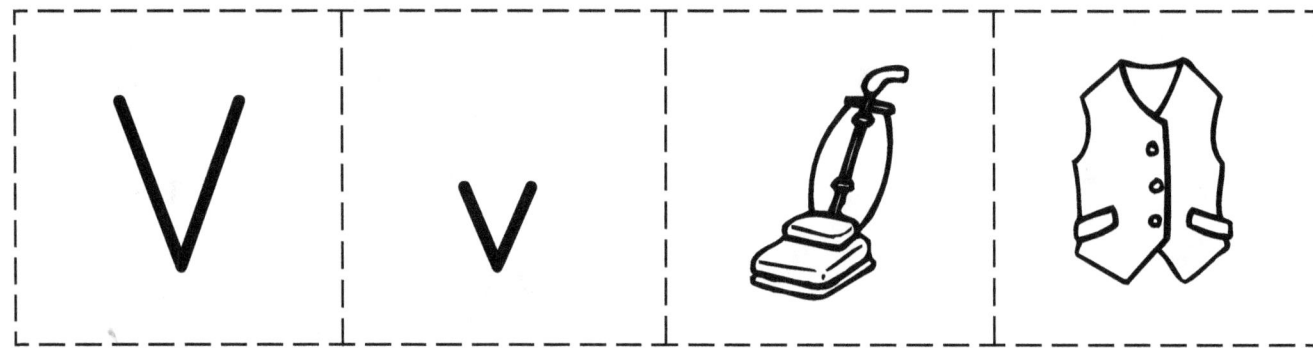

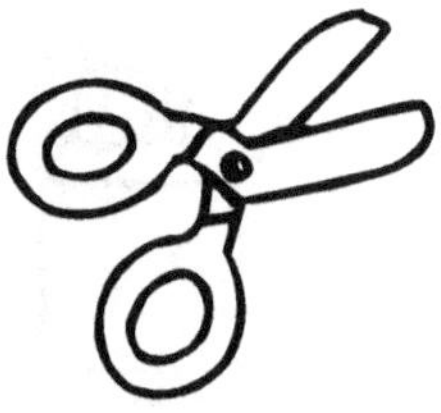

My
Cut and Paste
Alphabet Poster

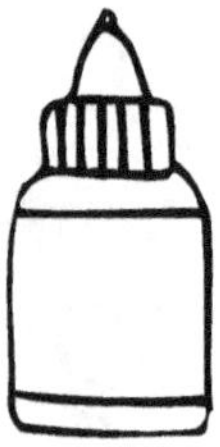

Name

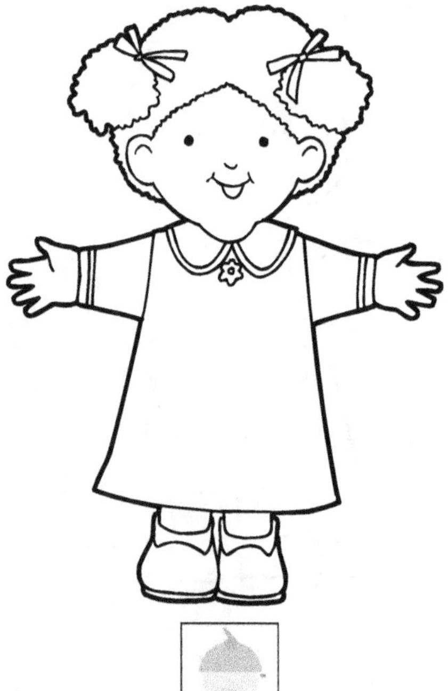

LAB201318 • ALPHABET CUT AND PASTE • 978-1-937257-36-1 •

Cut and Paste Alphabet Poster

W

w

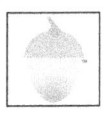

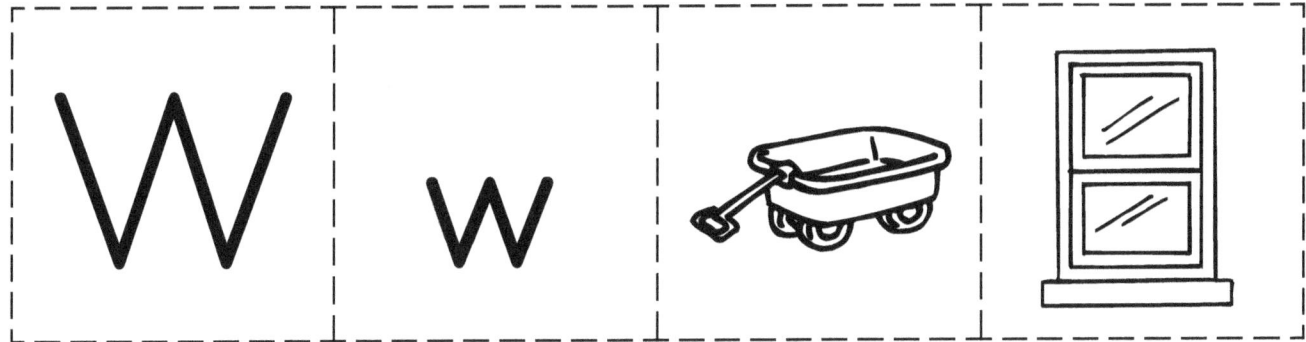

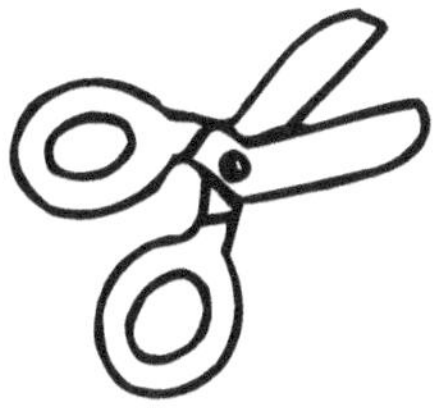

My Cut and Paste Alphabet Poster

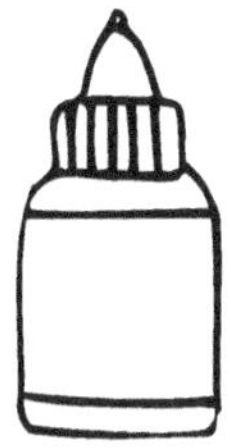

____

Name

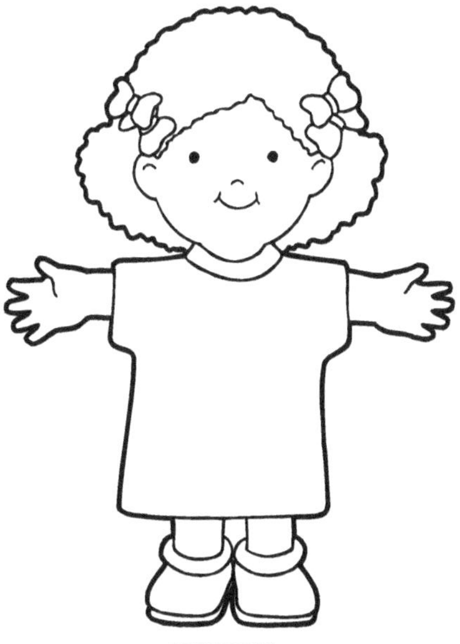

Cut and Paste Alphabet Poster

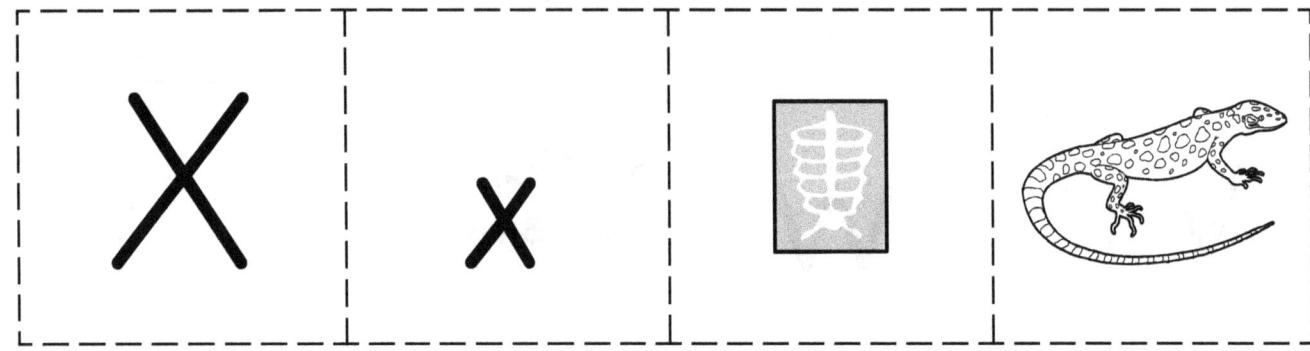

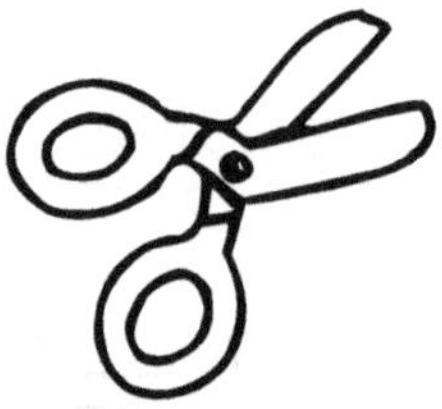

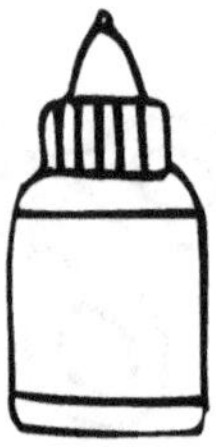

My
Cut and Paste
Alphabet Poster

_____
Name

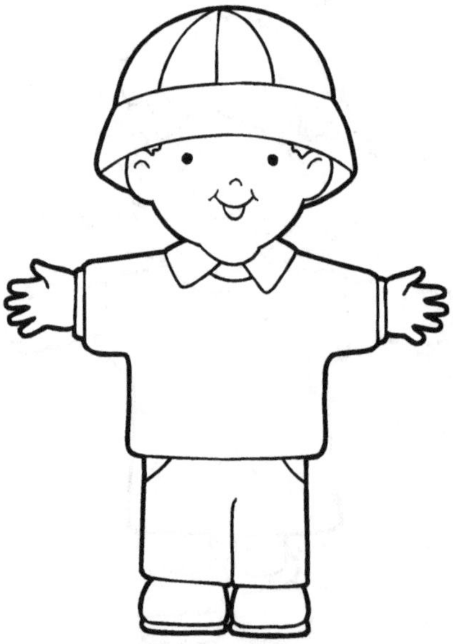

Cut and Paste Alphabet Poster

Y y

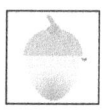

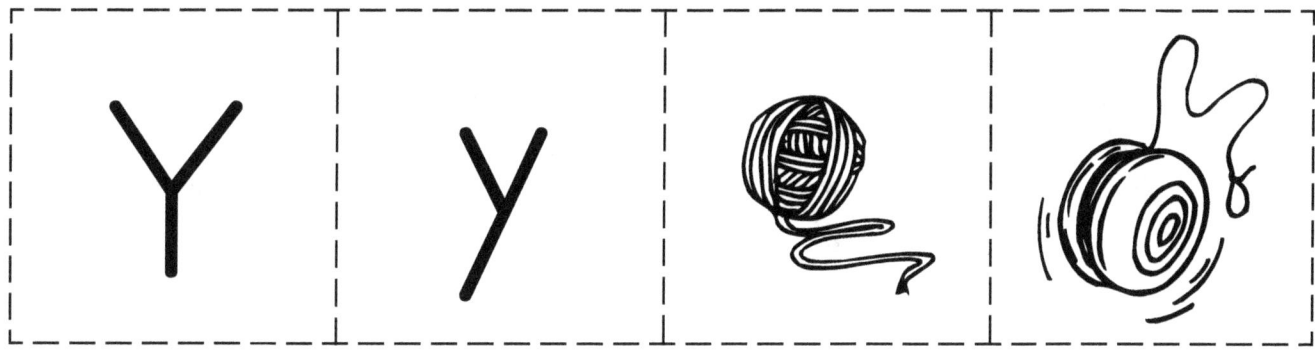

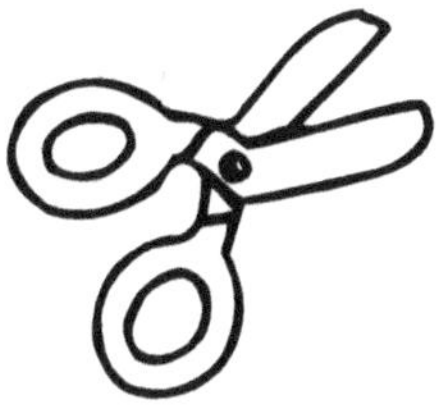

My Cut and Paste Alphabet Poster

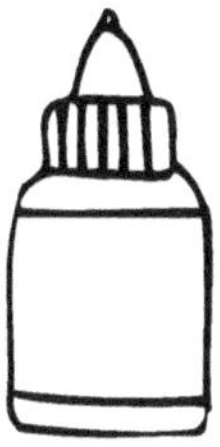

Name

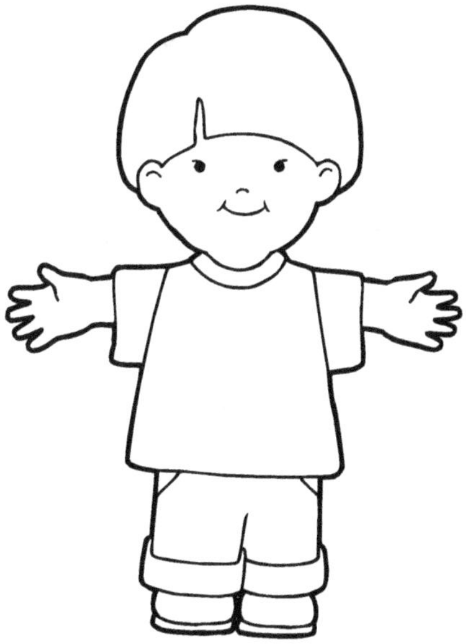

Cut and Paste Alphabet Poster

Z z

My Cut and Paste Alphabet Poster

Name

Cut and Paste Puzzles

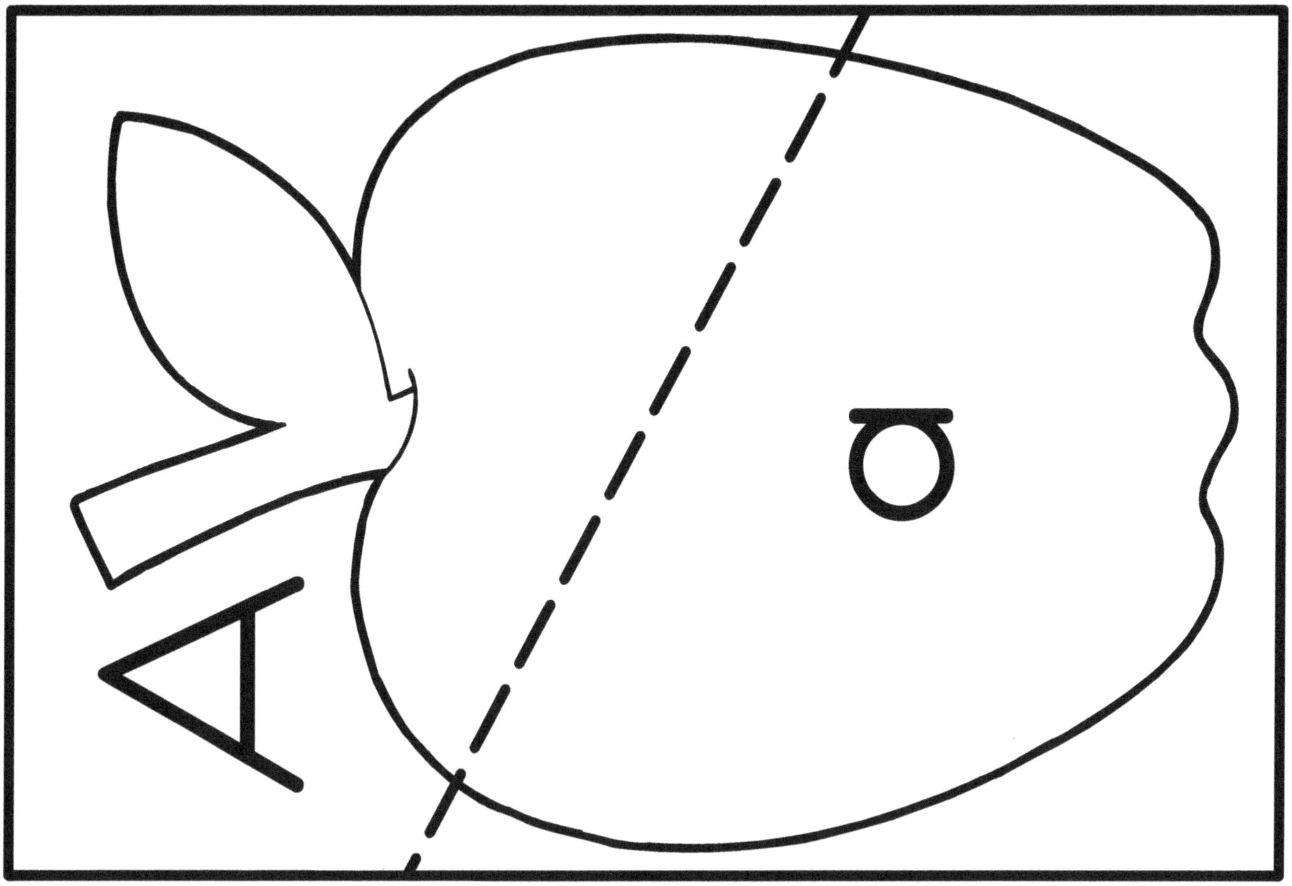

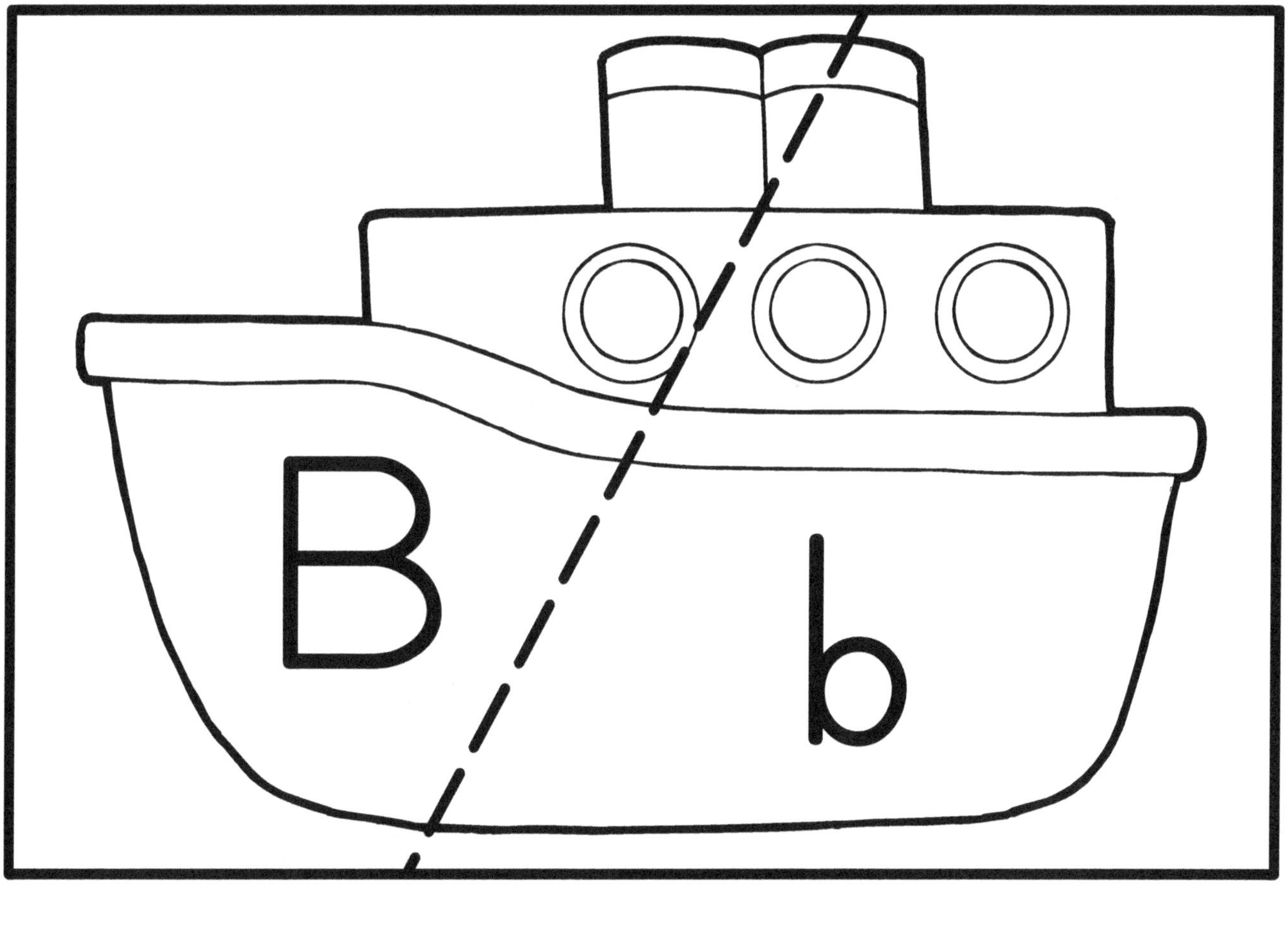

Cut and Paste Puzzles

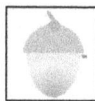

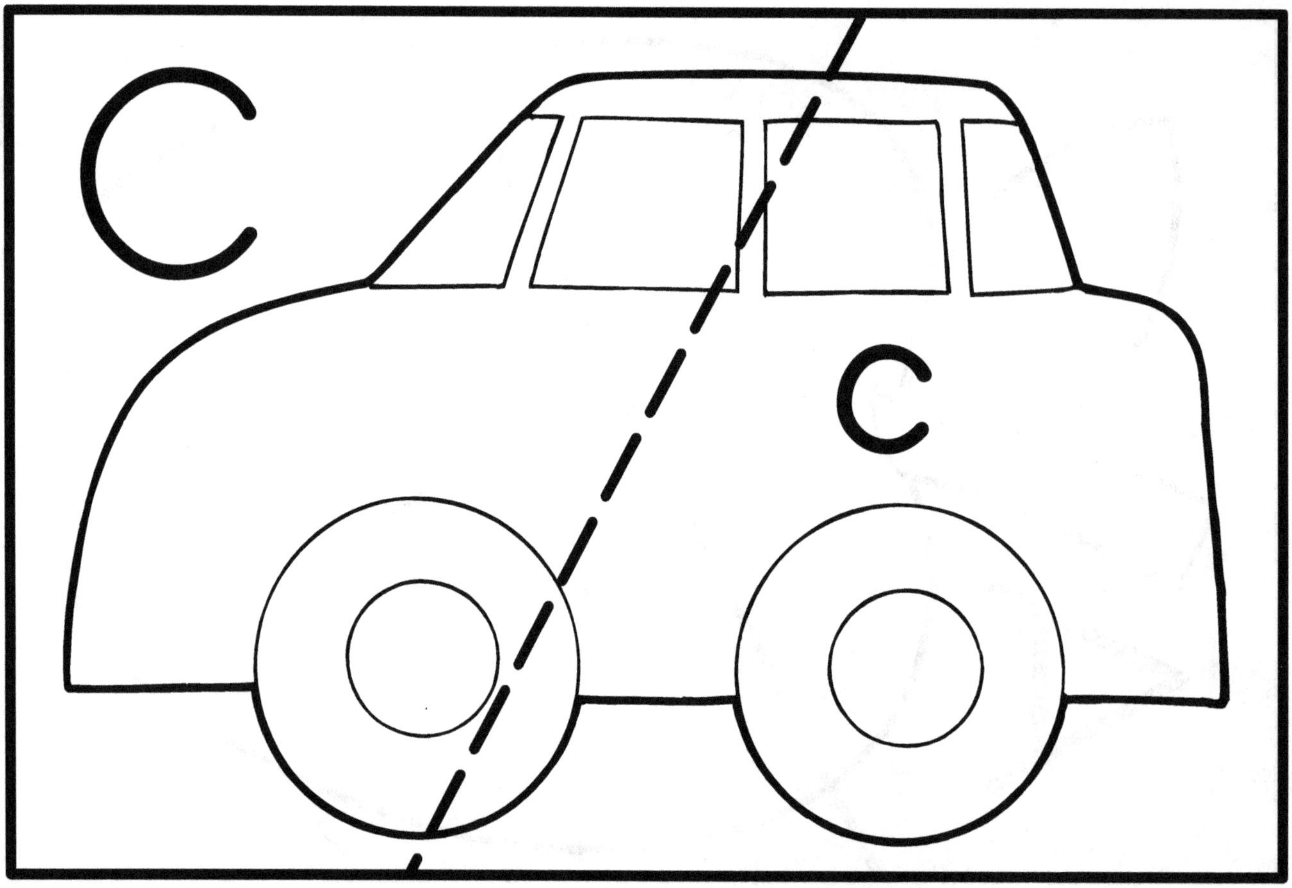

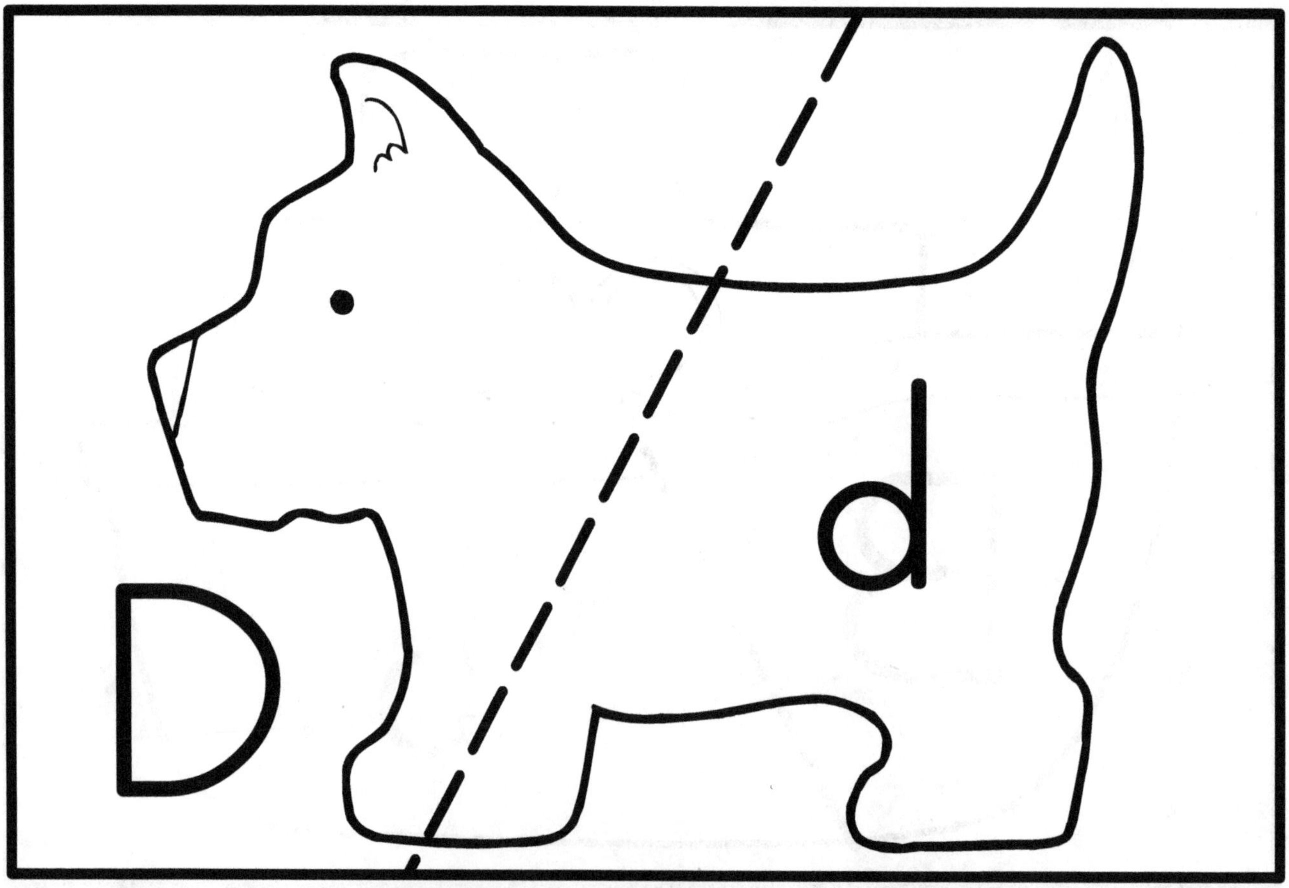

LAB201318 • ALPHABET CUT AND PASTE • 978-1-937257-36-1 •

Cut and Paste Puzzles

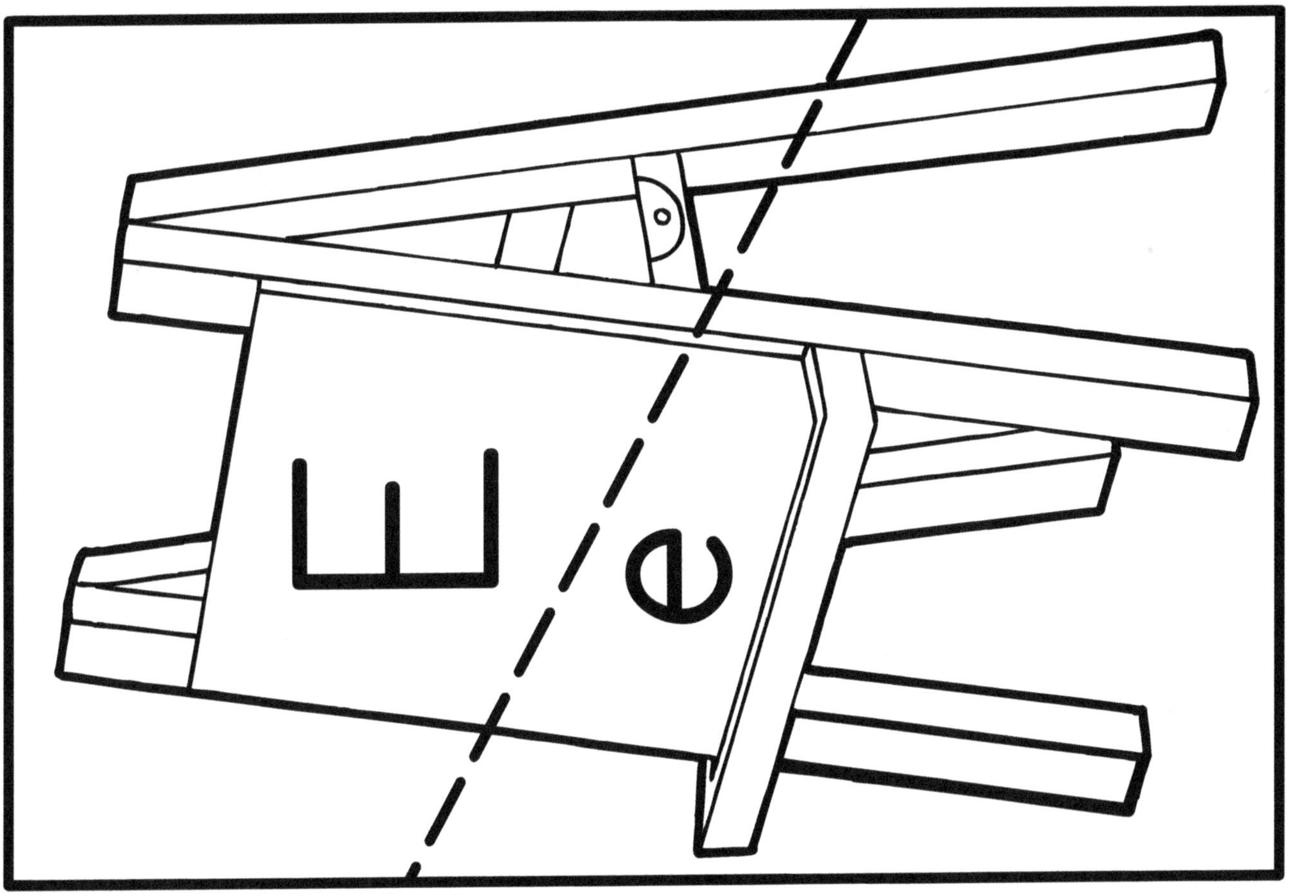

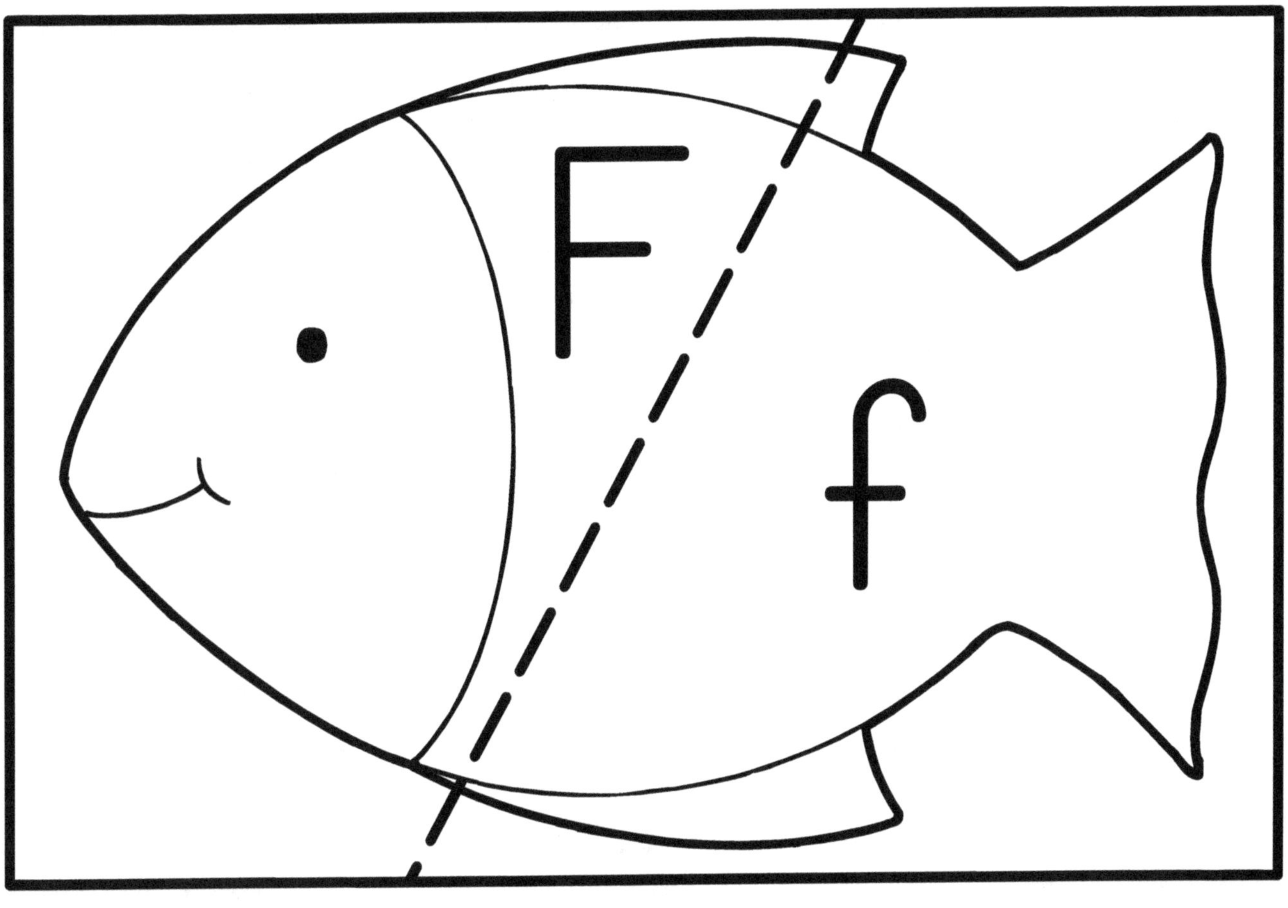

Cut and Paste Puzzles

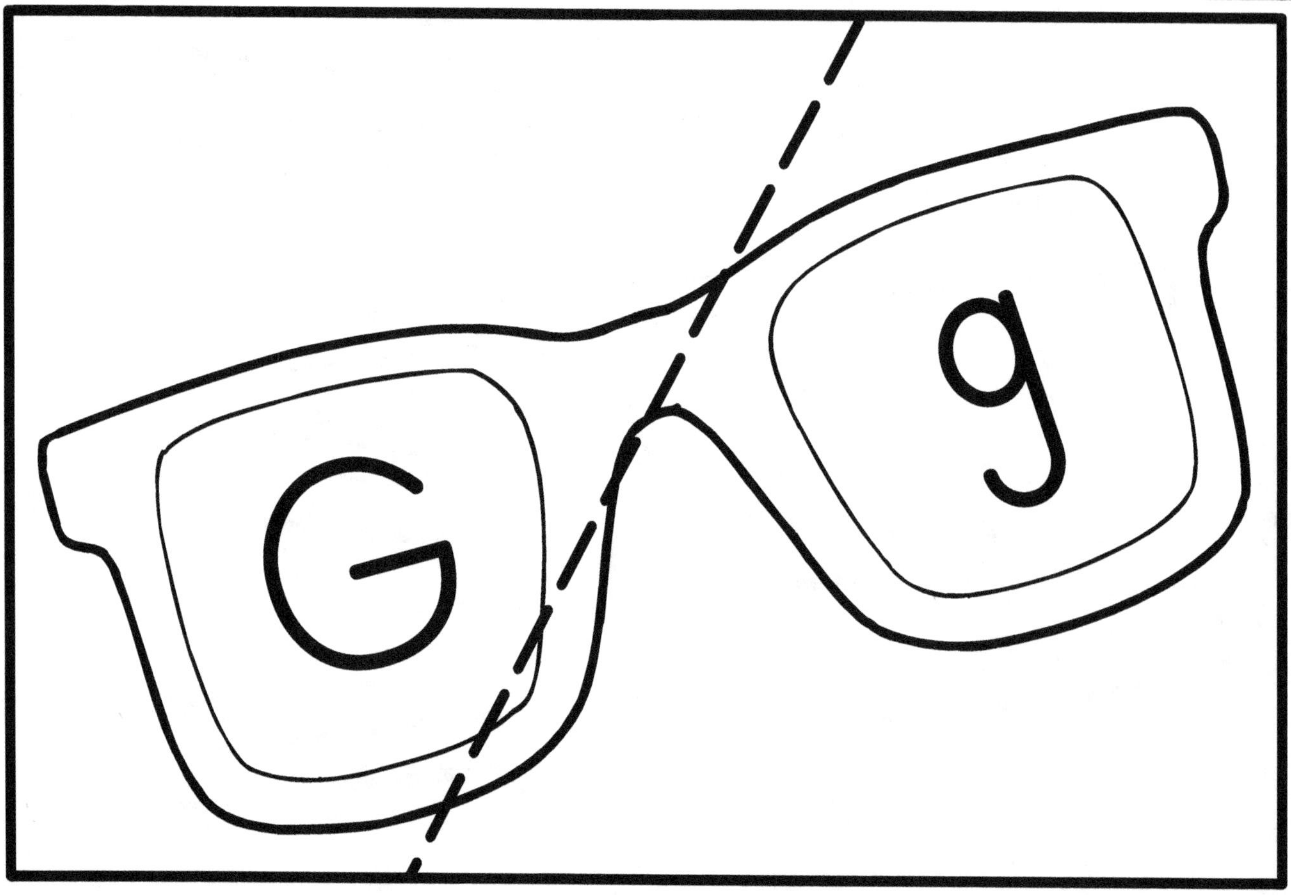

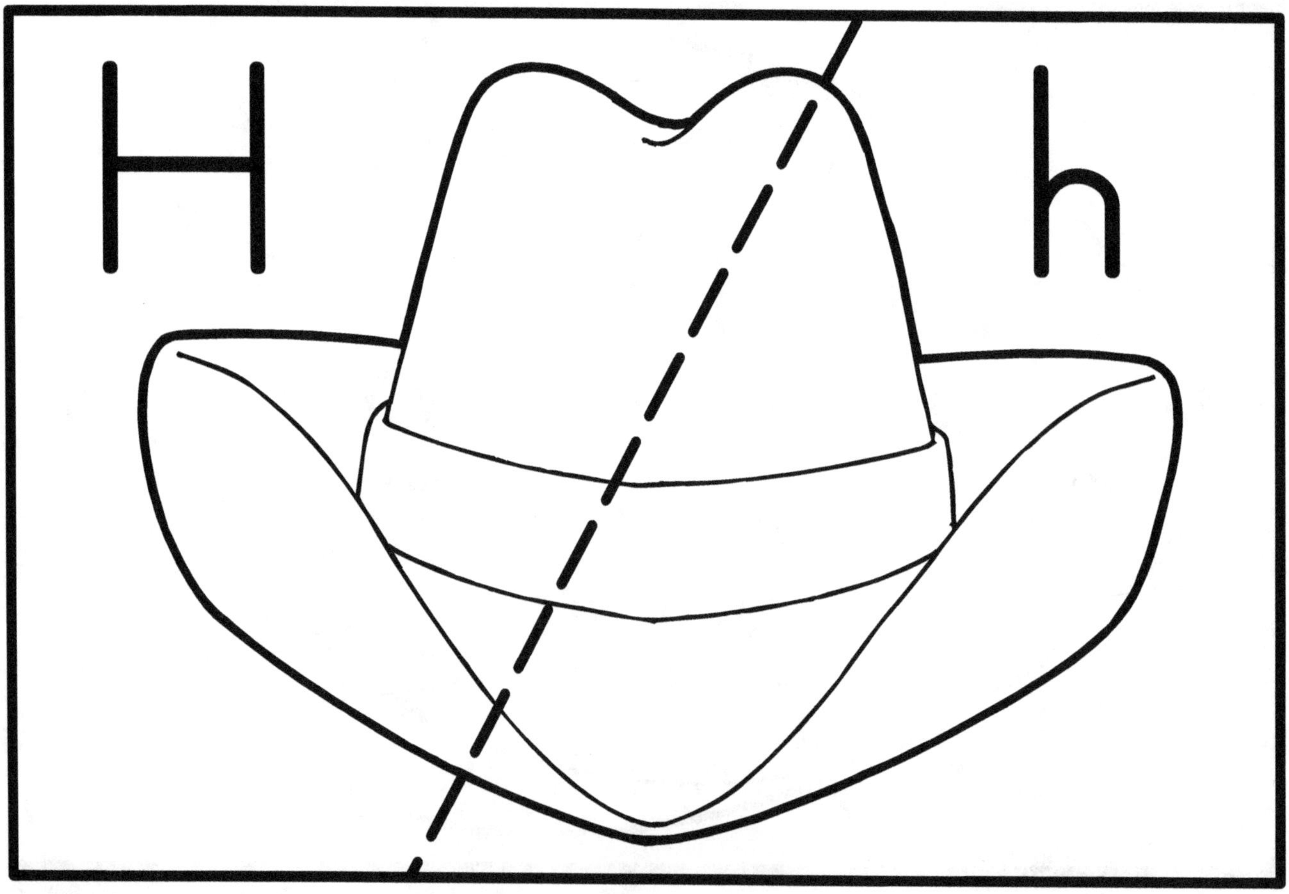

Cut and Paste Puzzles

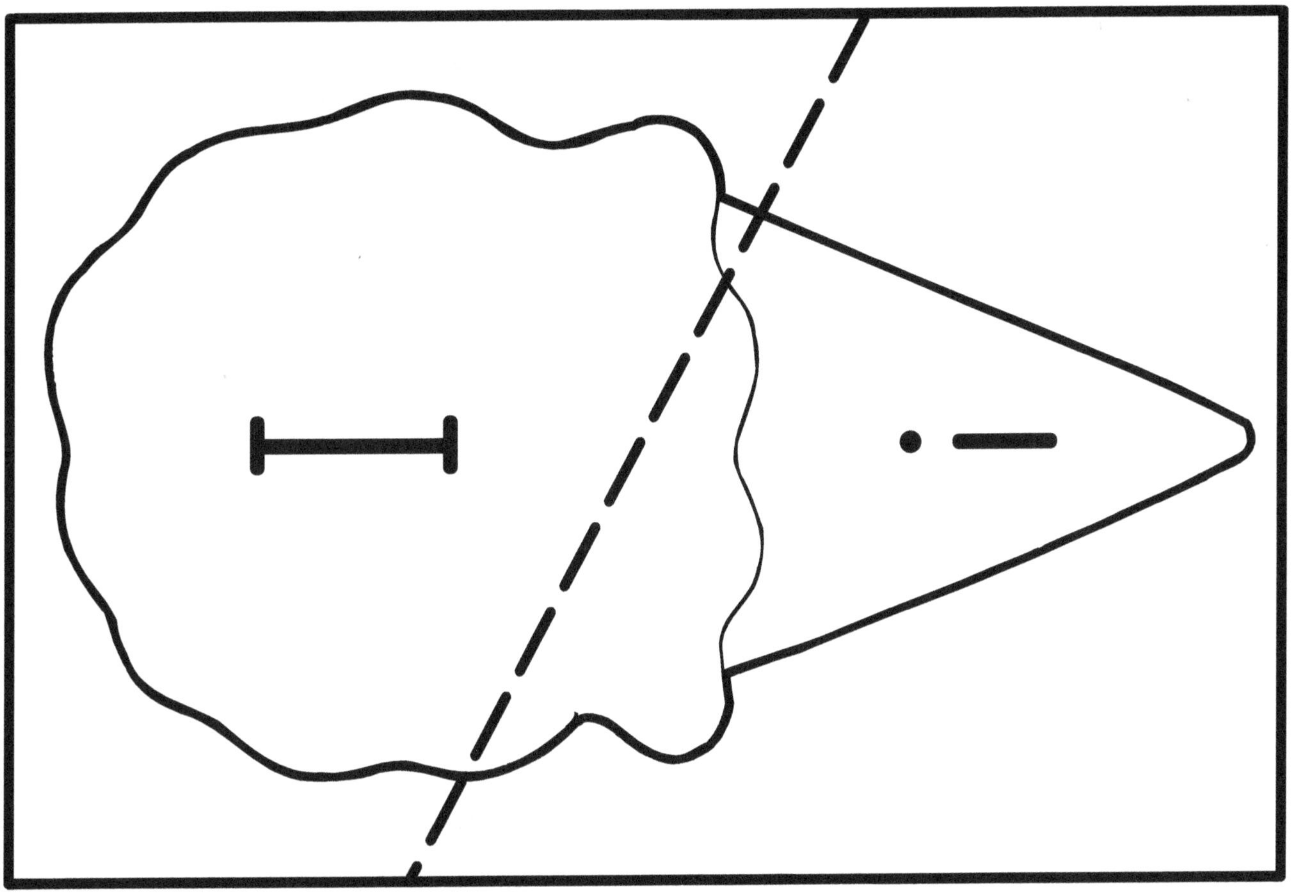

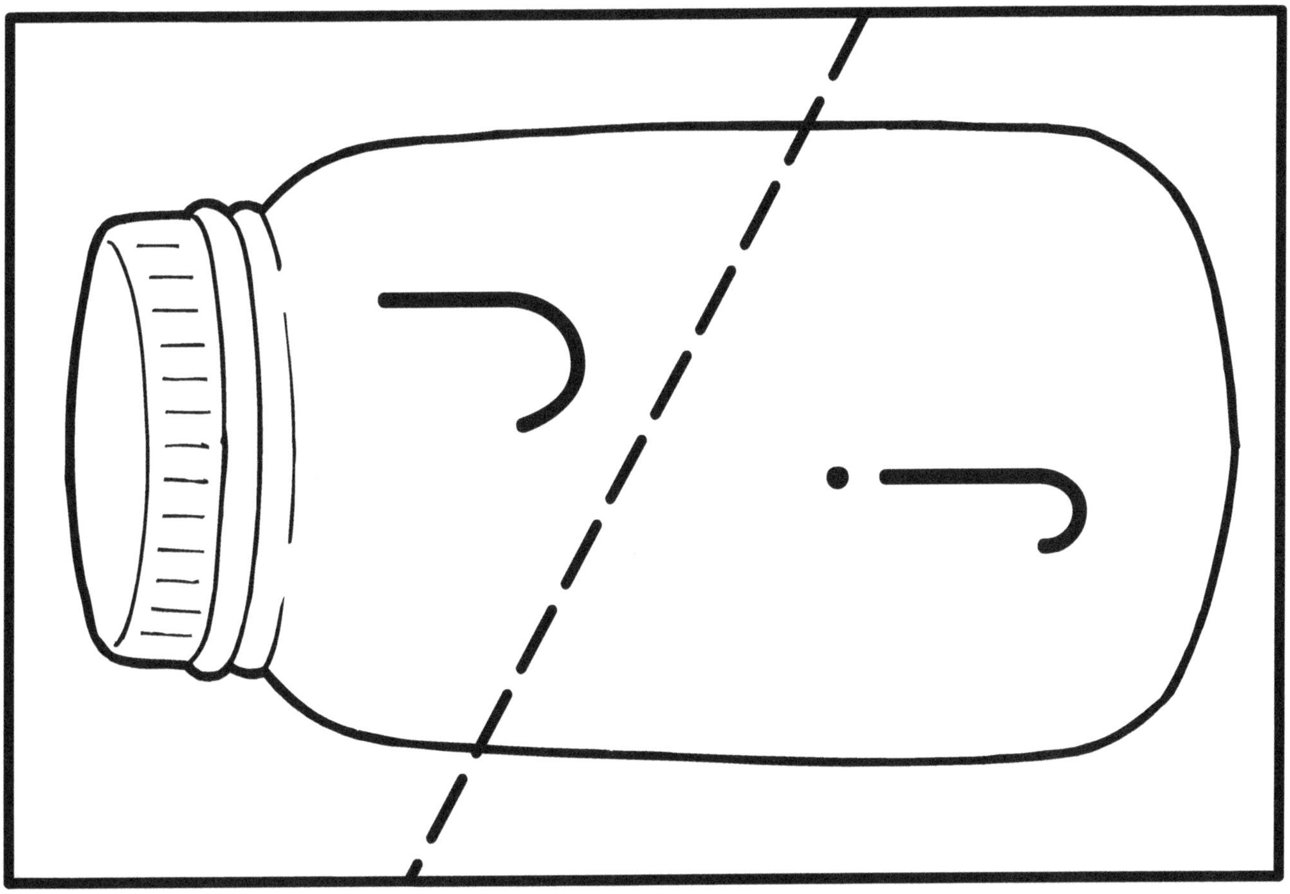

Cut and Paste Puzzles

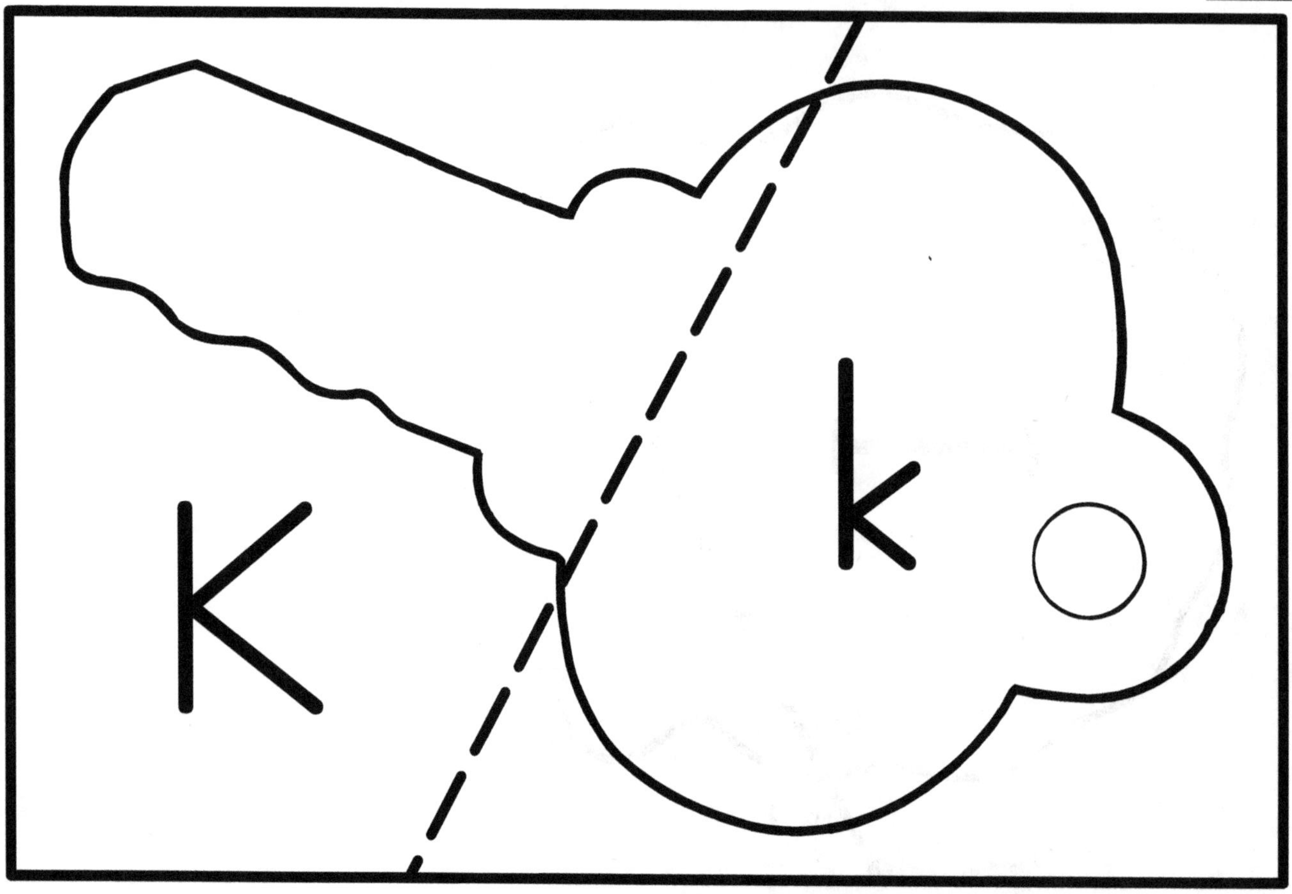

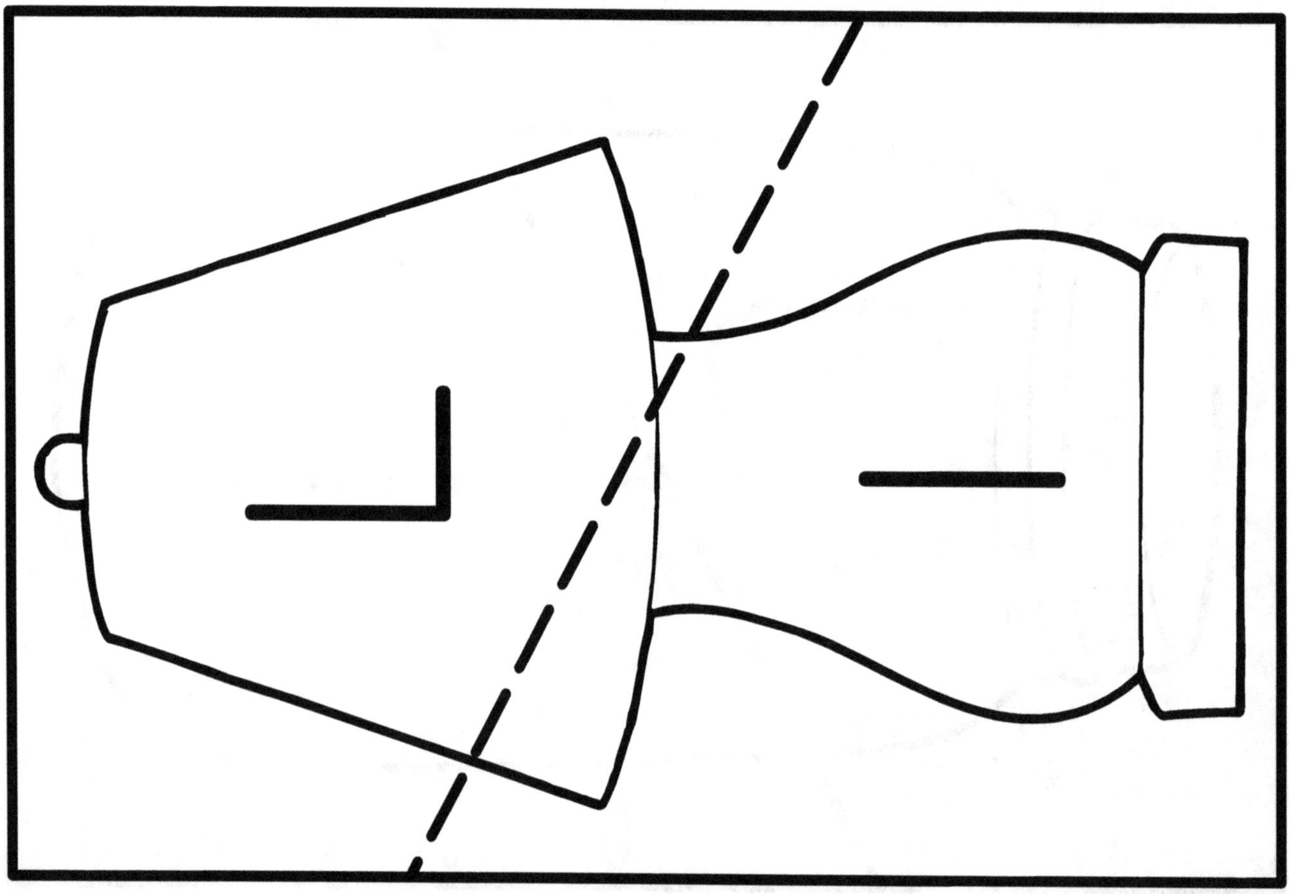

LAB201318 • ALPHABET CUT AND PASTE • 978-1-937257-36-1 •

Cut and Paste Puzzles

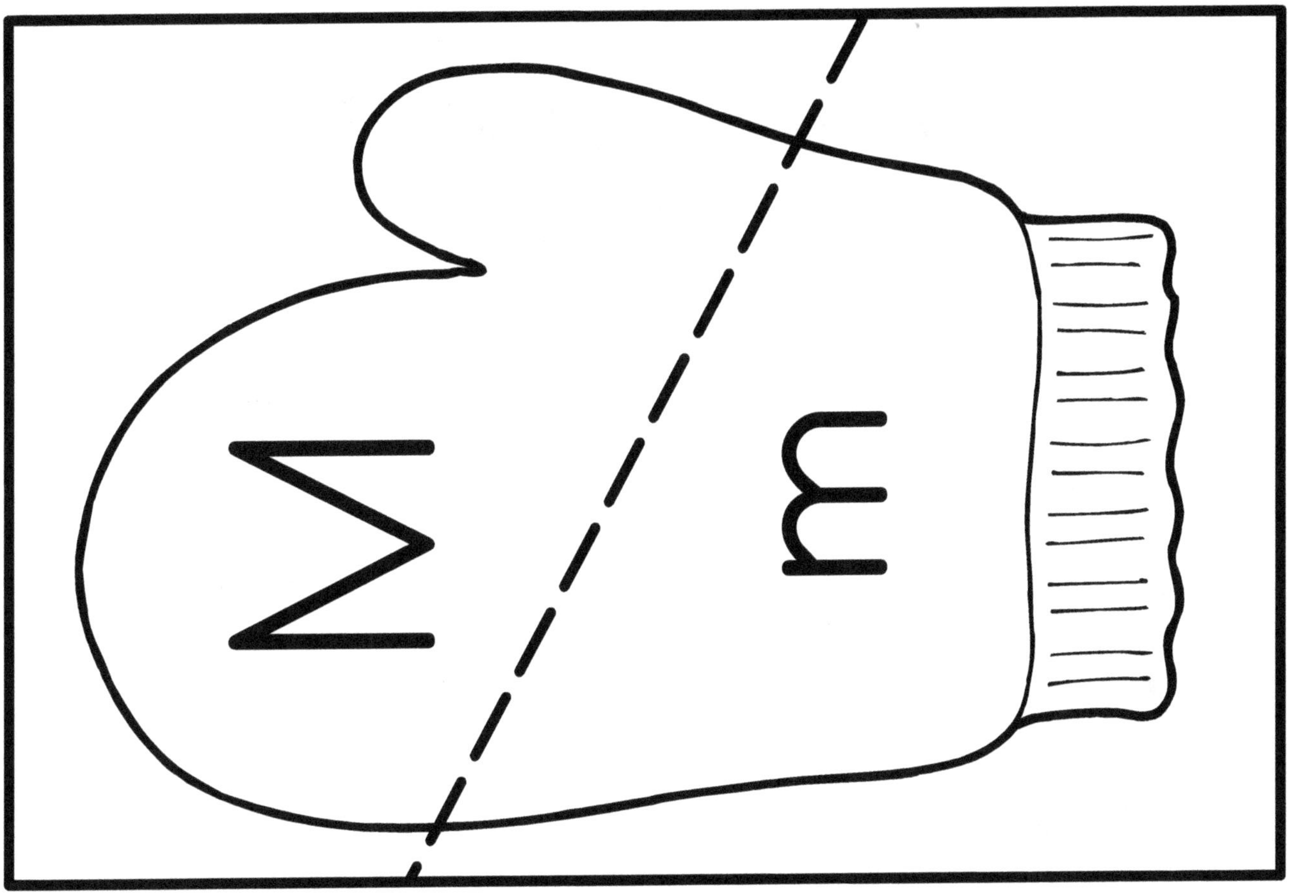

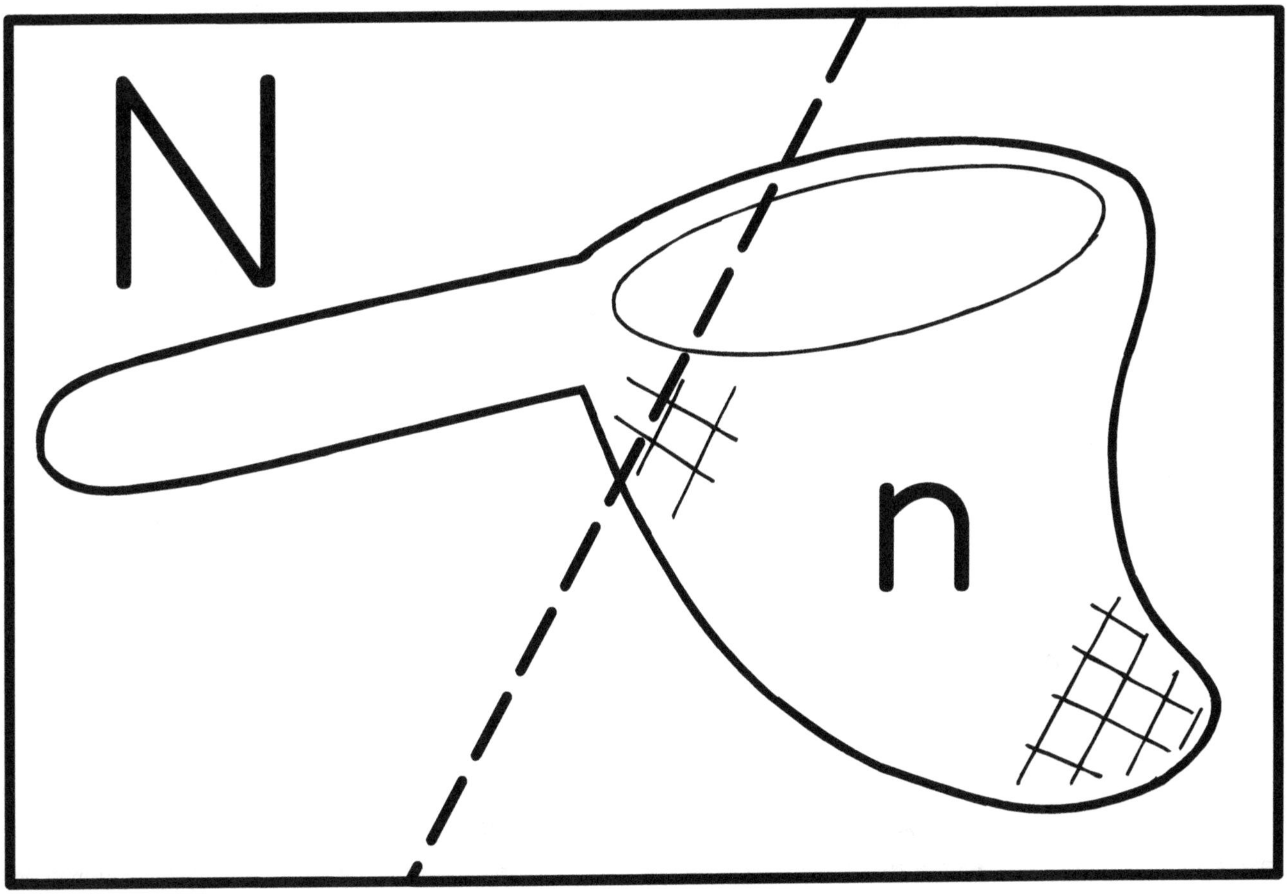

Cut and Paste Puzzles

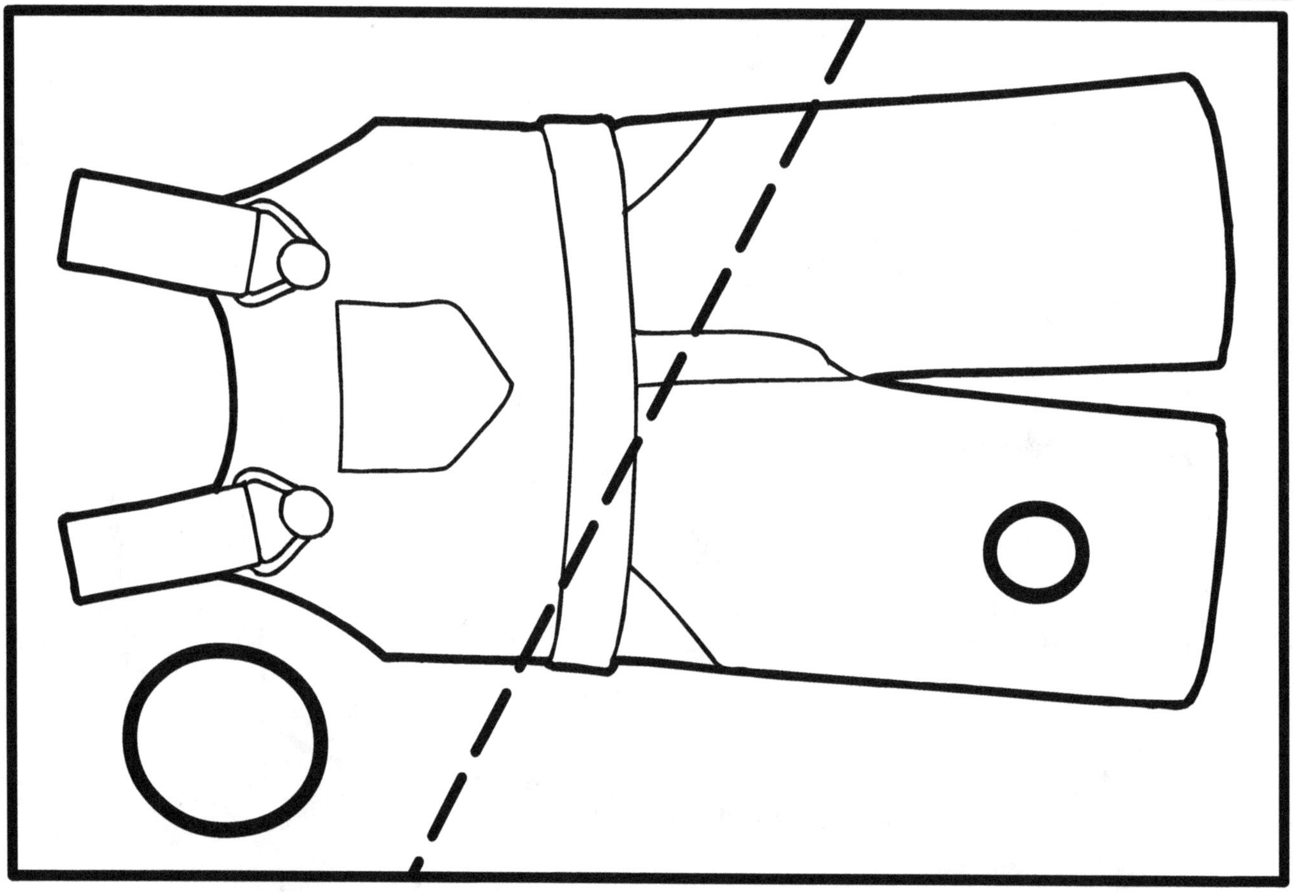

Cut and Paste Puzzles

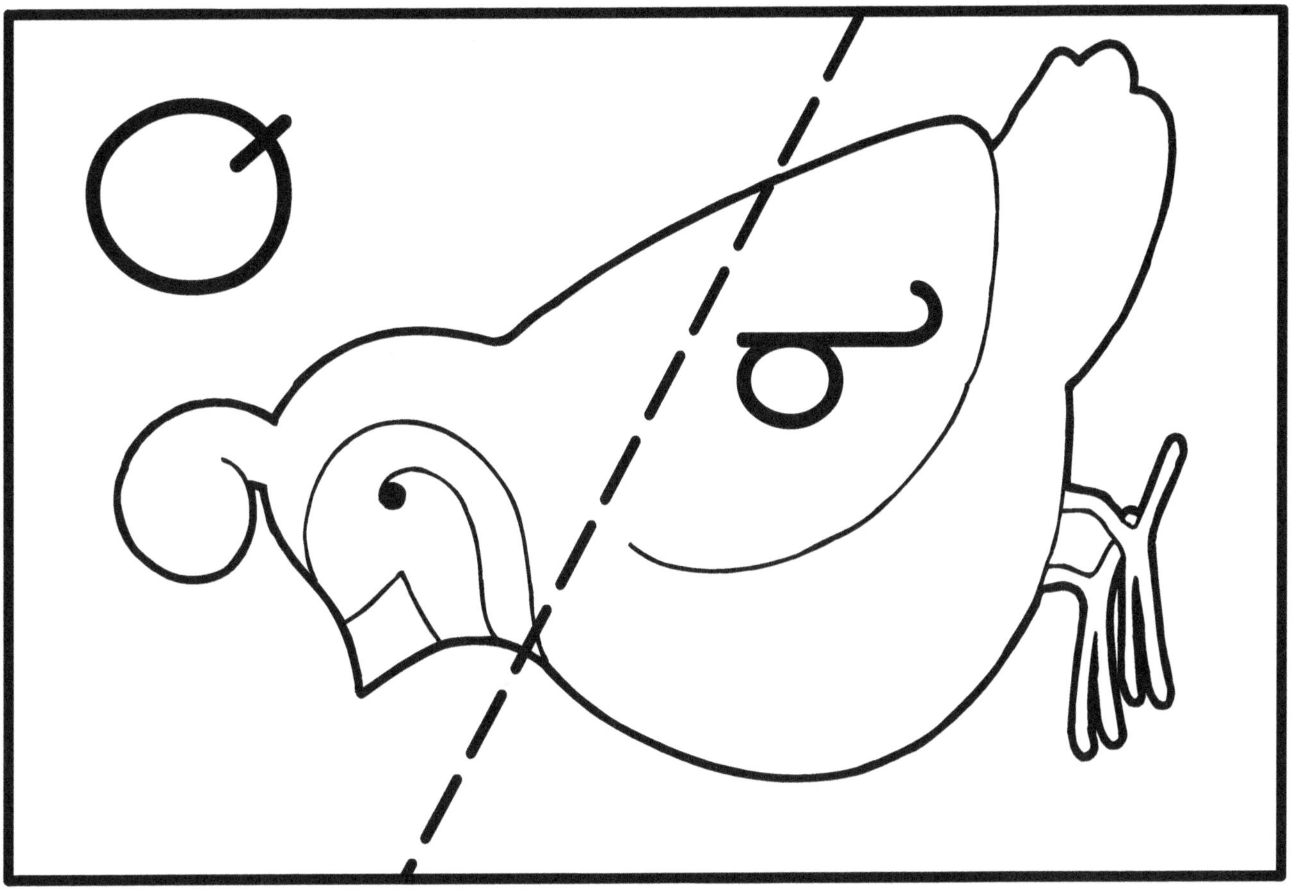

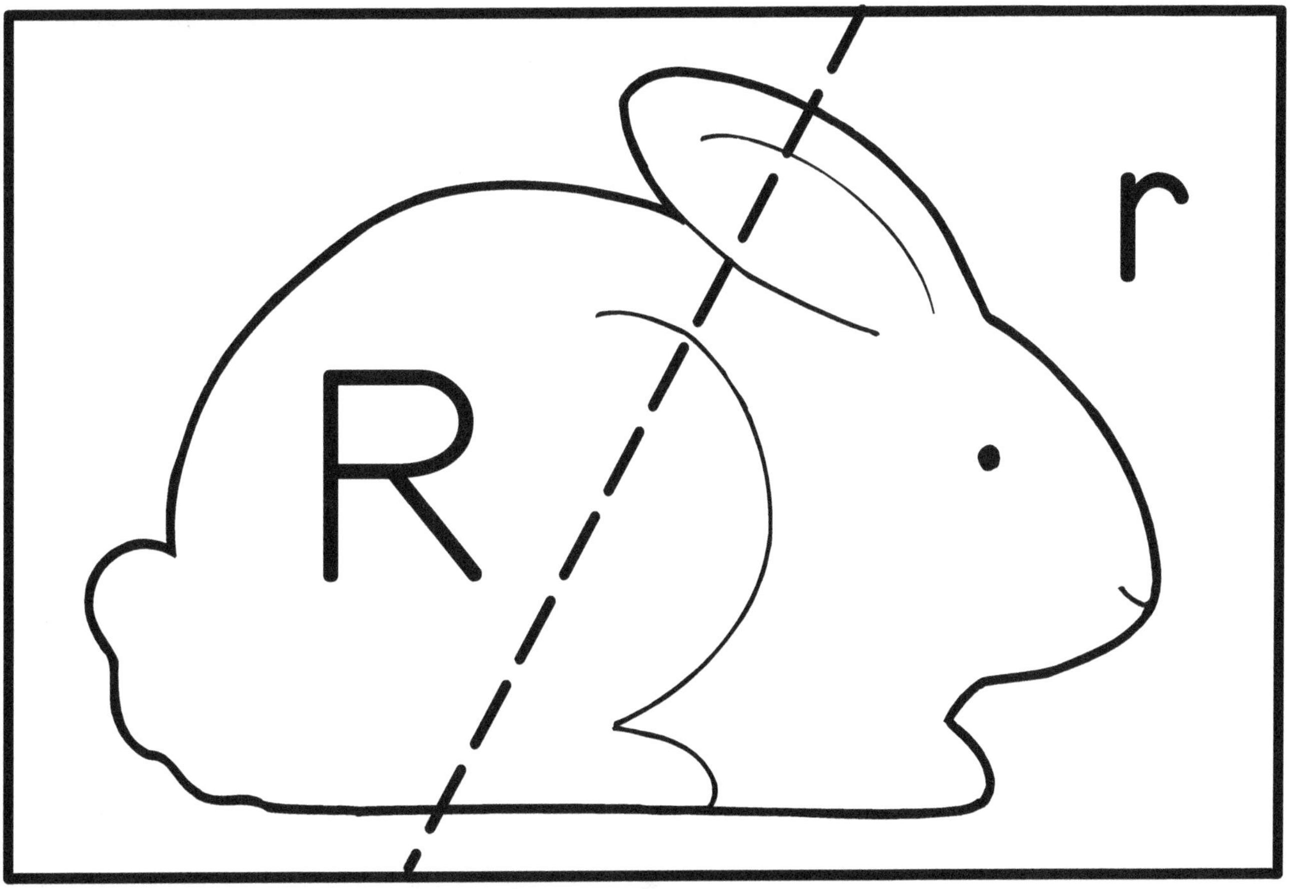

Cut and Paste Puzzles

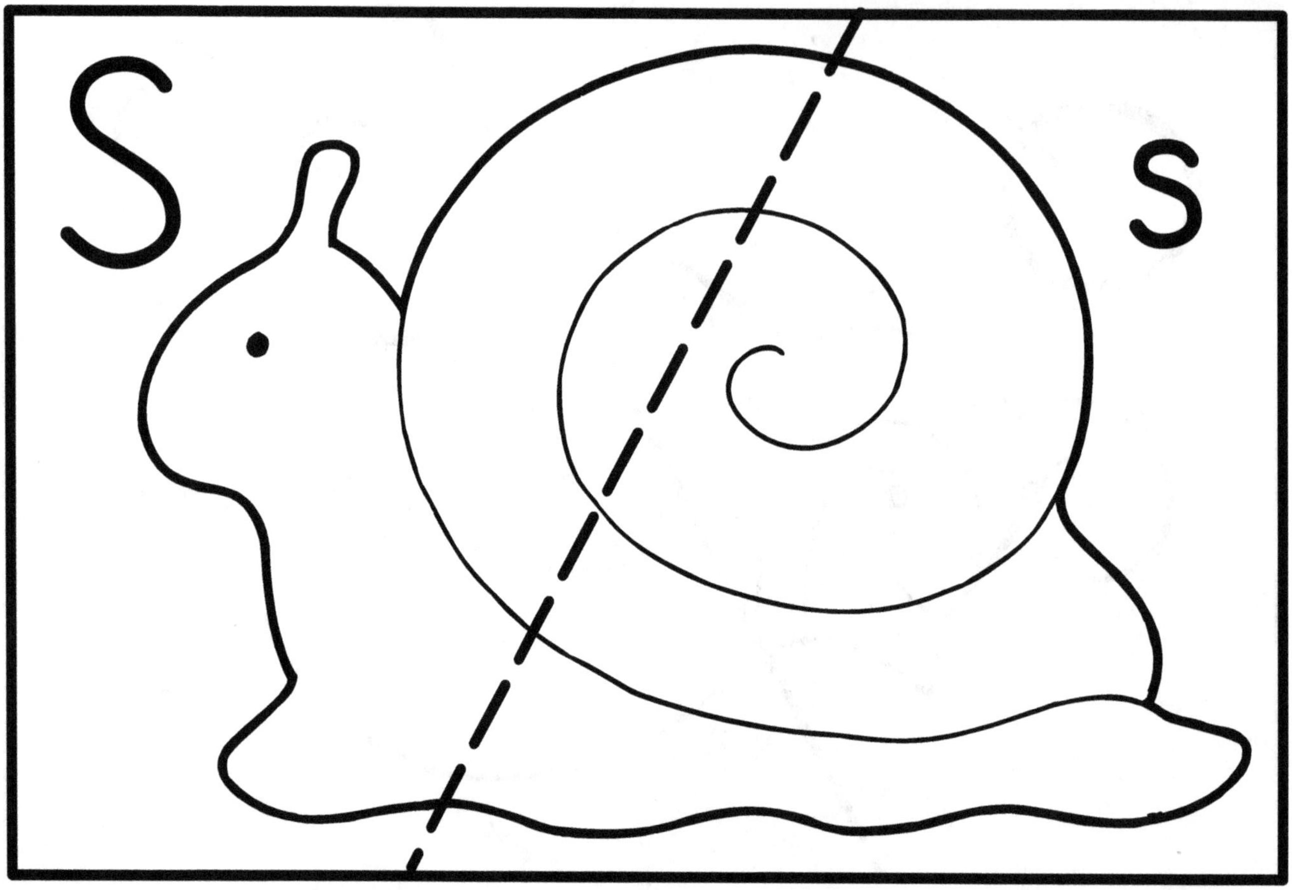

Cut and Paste Puzzles

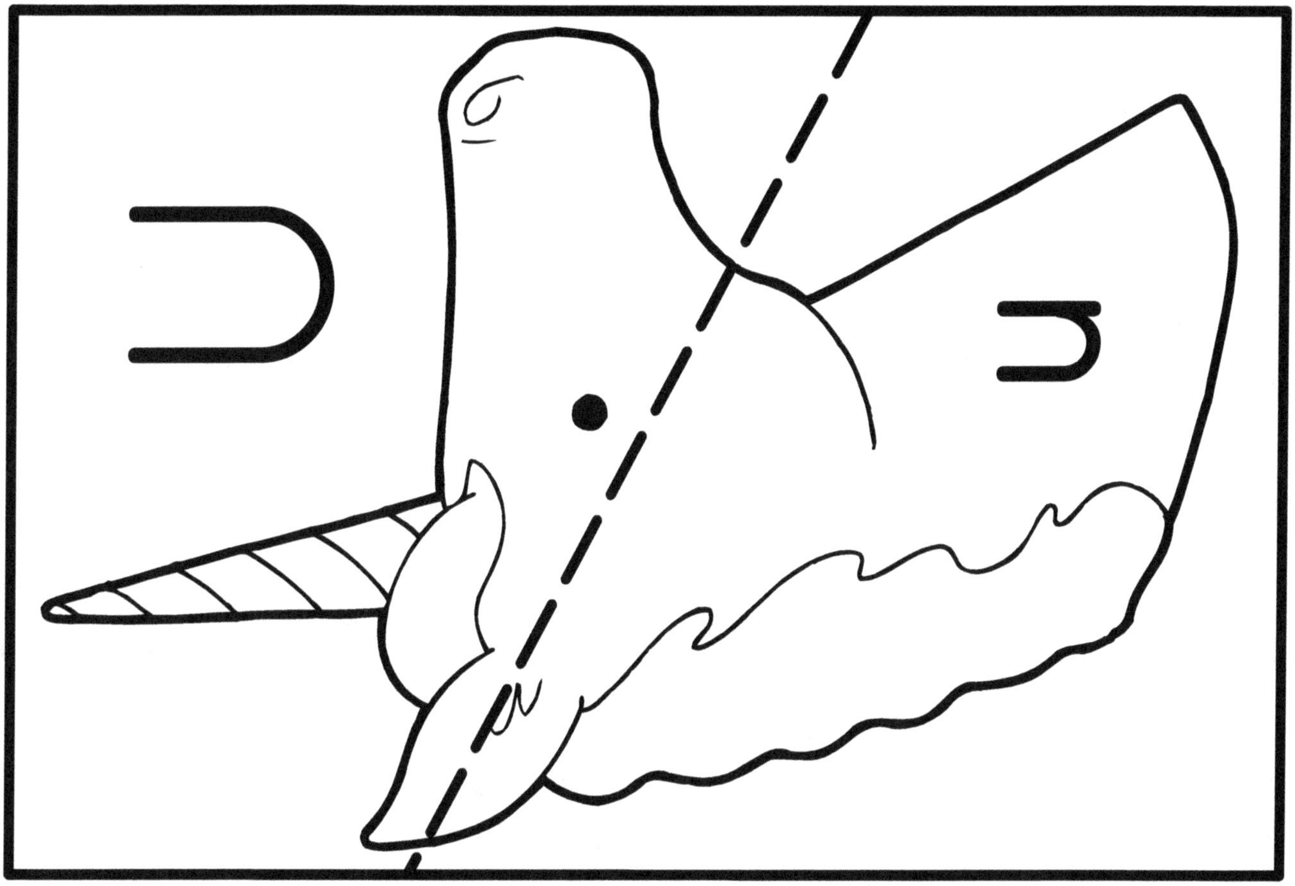

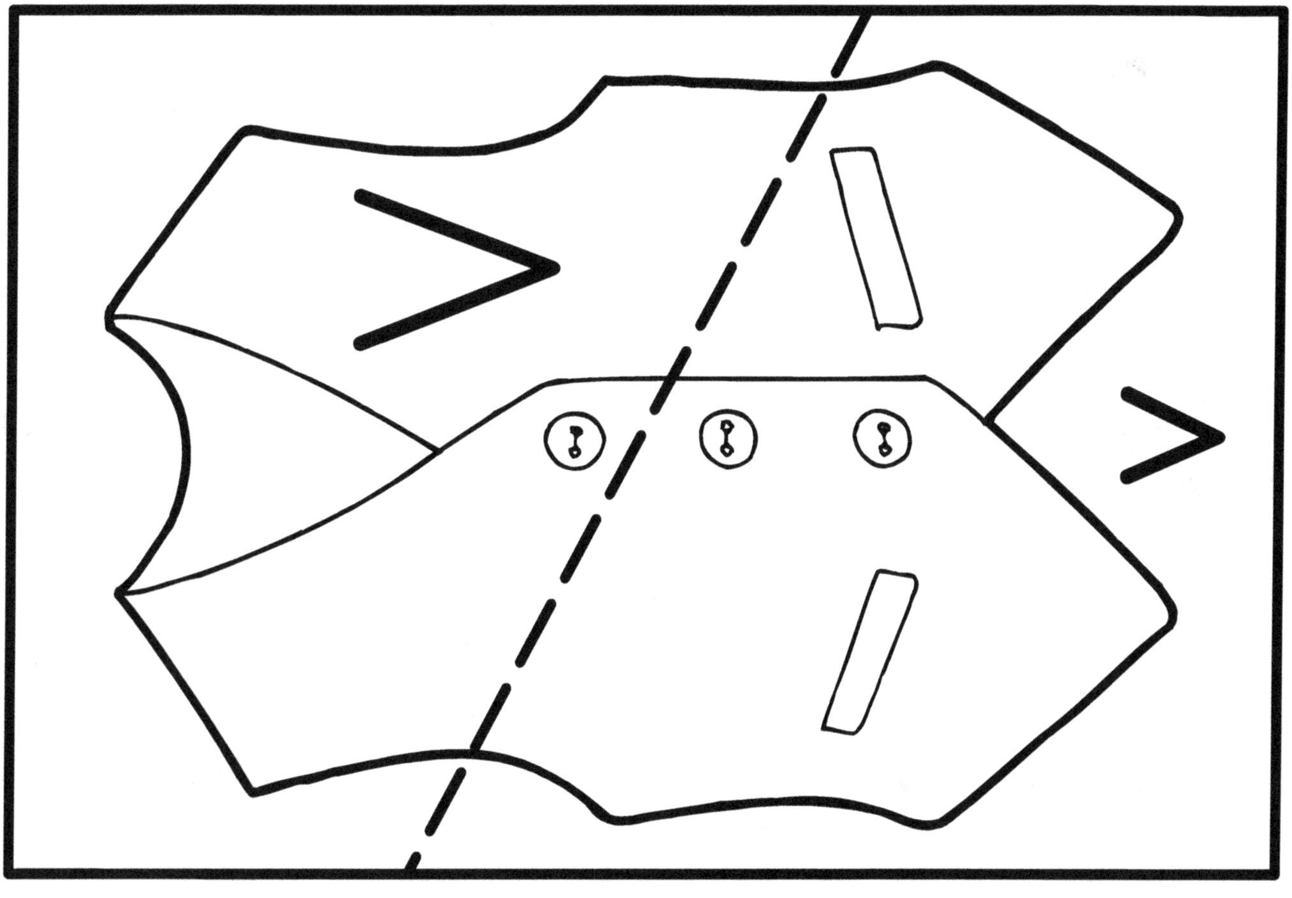

Cut and Paste Puzzles

Cut and Paste Puzzles

Puzzle Board

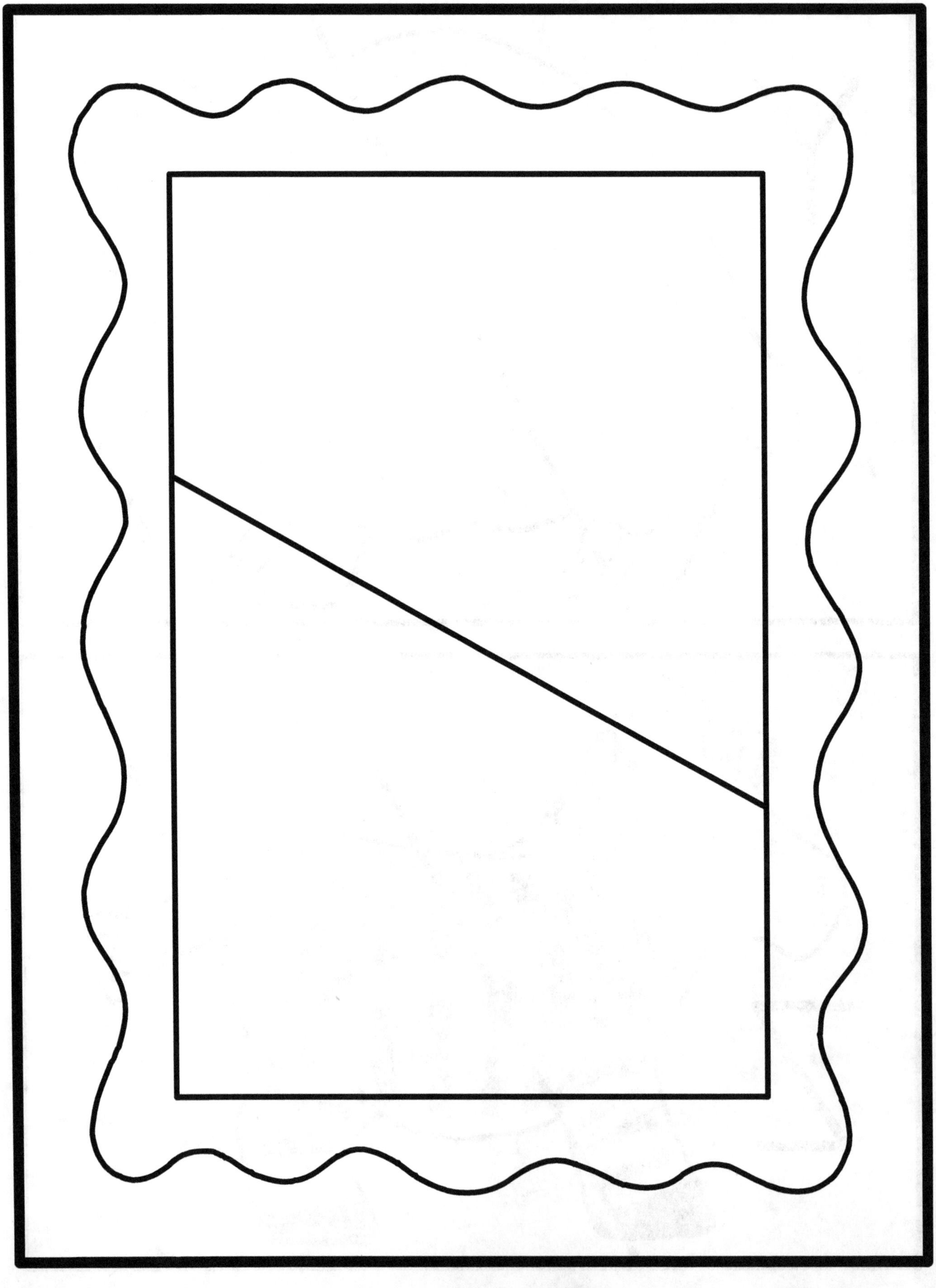

www.ingramcontent.com/pod-product-compliance
Lightning Source LLC
Chambersburg PA
CBHW081455060426
42444CB00037BA/3292